Contents

What is geography?   4

Chapter 1: Journey into the Earth   14
What the Earth itself is made of, how that all works, and how we find out more about it.

Chapter 2: Weather and climate   30
What goes on in the Earth's atmosphere, the difference between weather and climate, and how they both affect people's lives around the world.

Chapter 3: Watery world   44
All about oceans, rivers and ice – and how people's lives depend on water in all sorts of ways.

Chapter 4: Homes, towns, cities   56
Where people live, why they live there, and how people shape the places around them.

Chapter 5: How money and power shape the world   76
How countries and borders work, and how and why some countries are more powerful than others.

Chapter 6: Improving lives   92
Using the tools of geography to find out how people live in different countries and identify ways to improve lives.

Chapter 7: Big issues   100
What are some of the big questions that geographers ask?
What geography mysteries are yet to be solved?

Geography is *EVERYWHERE!*   120

Glossary   122

Jobs in geography   124

Index   126

Acknowledgements   128

Hurricane seen from above

Usborne Quicklinks
For links to websites where you can find out more about geography and explore some of the topics in this book with exciting videos and activities, and challenge yourself with puzzles and quizzes, go to **usborne.com/Quicklinks** and type in the title of the book.

Please follow the internet safety guidelines at Usborne Quicklinks. Children should be supervised online.

What is geography?

Geography is about people and places and how people and places interact with each other. Why are some parts of the world deserts, while others are forests? Why do people build cities in certain places? How does a landscape affect the people who live in it?

Now, imagine some friendly aliens are looking down on Earth from space...

Oh look! That planet looks different from the others.

I wonder if it contains any super-intelligent life forms, like us?

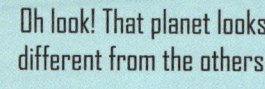

If it does, I wonder what they do and how they live?

Let's find out! Prepare for landing.

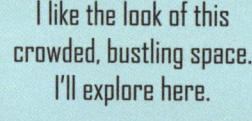

I like the look of this crowded, bustling space. I'll explore here.

It's so loud! I want to find somewhere green and quiet.

Looking at the world from an alien's point of view is one way to think like a geographer.

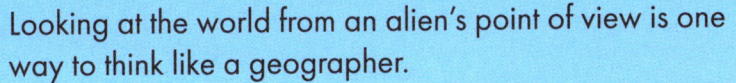

"Why have you built your houses on top of these hills?"

"To avoid river flooding, and a nasty disease that people catch from the marshy area by the riverbank. And from the hills, we can see what's happening far away, which makes us feel safe."

"But why *these* particular hills?"

"Because this is where the river is easiest to cross. It's quick and easy to travel to other places, and trade with them, too."

"Any other reason?"

"Actually, yes. A nearby volcano made the soil fertile so we can grow olive trees and grapevines. We can even use ash from the volcano to make concrete."

Finding out *why* people end up living *where* they do, and *what kind* of work or industries develop in different areas, is all part of geography.

"Any plans for the future?"

"Well, some people are moving to lower ground, where it's more sheltered from all the wild storms of recent years. The plan is to drain the marshes, and find a way to guard against floods."

"Aha! So geography is also about how people are *changing* because of the planet, and how the planet is changing because of people."

Geography connects to everything

In real life, geography often starts with a question. These questions can cover a huge range of overlapping topics. Different kinds of geographers focus on different areas.

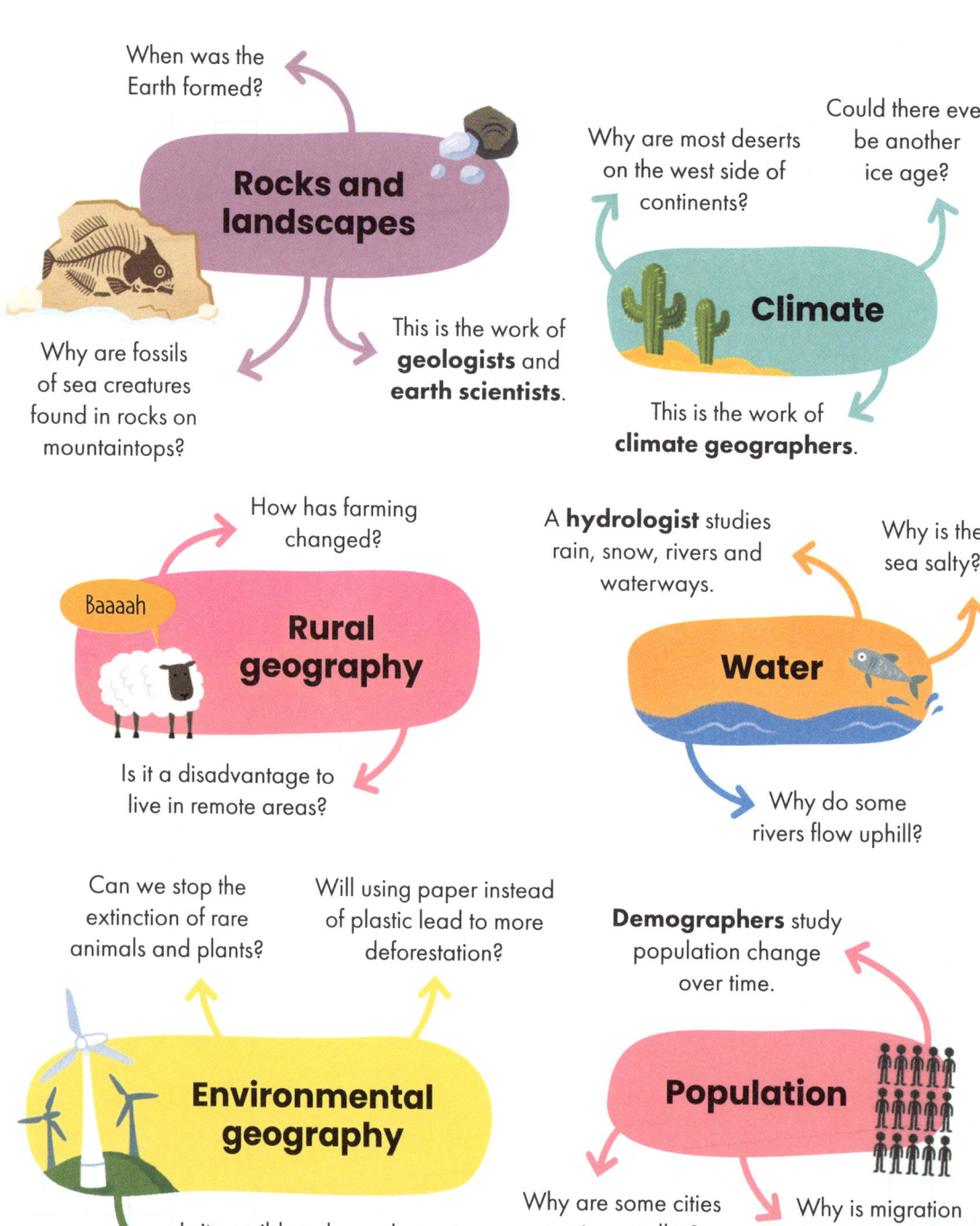

When was the Earth formed?

Rocks and landscapes

Why are fossils of sea creatures found in rocks on mountaintops?

This is the work of **geologists** and **earth scientists**.

Why are most deserts on the west side of continents?

Could there ever be another ice age?

Climate

This is the work of **climate geographers**.

How has farming changed?

Baaaah

Rural geography

Is it a disadvantage to live in remote areas?

A **hydrologist** studies rain, snow, rivers and waterways.

Why is the sea salty?

Water

Why do some rivers flow uphill?

Can we stop the extinction of rare animals and plants?

Will using paper instead of plastic lead to more deforestation?

Environmental geography

Is it possible to have clean air and thriving industries?

Demographers study population change over time.

Population

Why are some cities getting smaller?

Why is migration increasing so fast?

How do restaurants and coffee shops change areas?

I see! ALL of this is geography.

Urban geography

How do languages spread around the world?

Should we protect green spaces instead of building new homes?

Where do people want to live?

Culture and society

Why do more people live on their own in some countries than in others?

What causes an ice storm?

What exactly is a *country*?

Weather

Political geography

How far ahead can we predict storms and floods?

This is the work of **climatologists** and **meteorologists**.

How are oil and conflict connected?

Why do borders change?

How can governments prevent poverty?

Where are new technology companies based?

Development

Economic geography

Why does life expectancy vary so much between countries?

How important are high-speed railways?

7

What geographers do

Geographers go out and visit all kinds of places. They look at what's happening and try to work out how and why things are changing. This often involves some science, but also exploring a place and asking questions.

Geographers try to find answers to all their questions by collecting information, known as **data**. They do this in lots of different ways.

Talking to people

How long have you lived here?

Survey
How has the village changed in the last 20 years?

Measuring things

I wonder how polluted the air in this sample is?

Counting things

How many people are shopping at noon?

Making sketches and taking notes

Geographers also look for data in books, newspapers and magazines, in public records in libraries and on the internet.

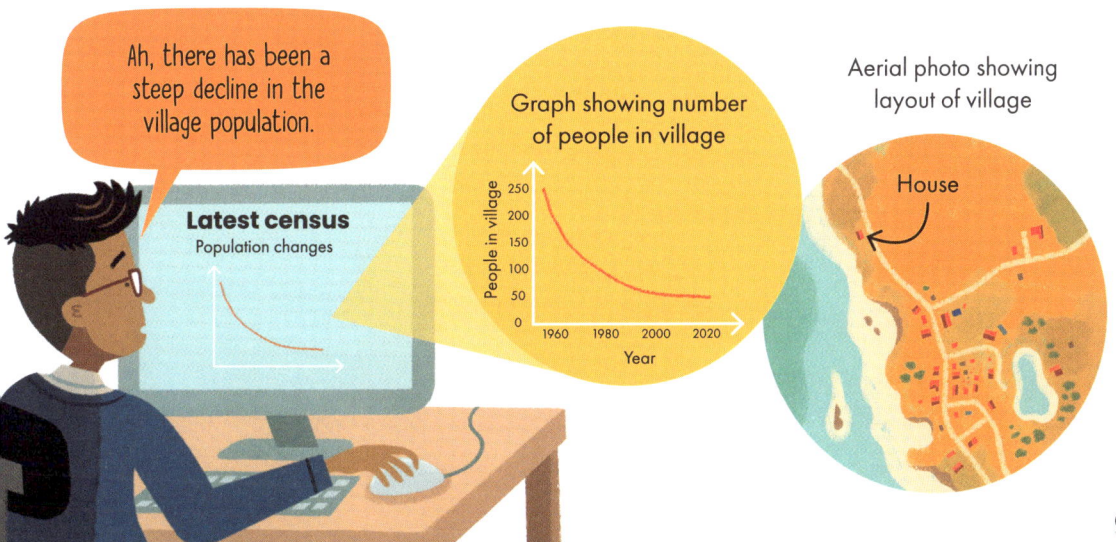

Ah, there has been a steep decline in the village population.

Latest census
Population changes

Graph showing number of people in village

People in village / Year

Aerial photo showing layout of village

House

Mapping the world

Maps are an essential tool for geographers. They show clearly where things are. But the world is three-dimensional and maps are generally flat, so making an accurate map is not as easy as you might think.

Here are two different maps of planet Earth.

They look REALLY different!

Placing the Atlantic Ocean in the middle makes it seem more important than the Pacific Ocean, which is shown here split in two.

The way a map is arranged determines which places are emphasized more than others.

On this map, the South Pole is at the top, the Pacific Ocean in the middle, and the Atlantic Ocean is split in two.

Changing the view changes the way we see things in the world.

That's odd! On those world maps above, Greenland looks roughly the same size as Africa...

...but this globe shows better how big they *actually* are compared to each other. Africa is over 14 TIMES the size of Greenland.

Our planet can be represented in multiple ways and directions. How it's shown on a map ultimately depends on the mapmaker, and their own views, interests and choices.

Using maps

Maps are designed to show things in a clear, visual way, so people can read them easily. This means knowing what to put in, and what to leave out.

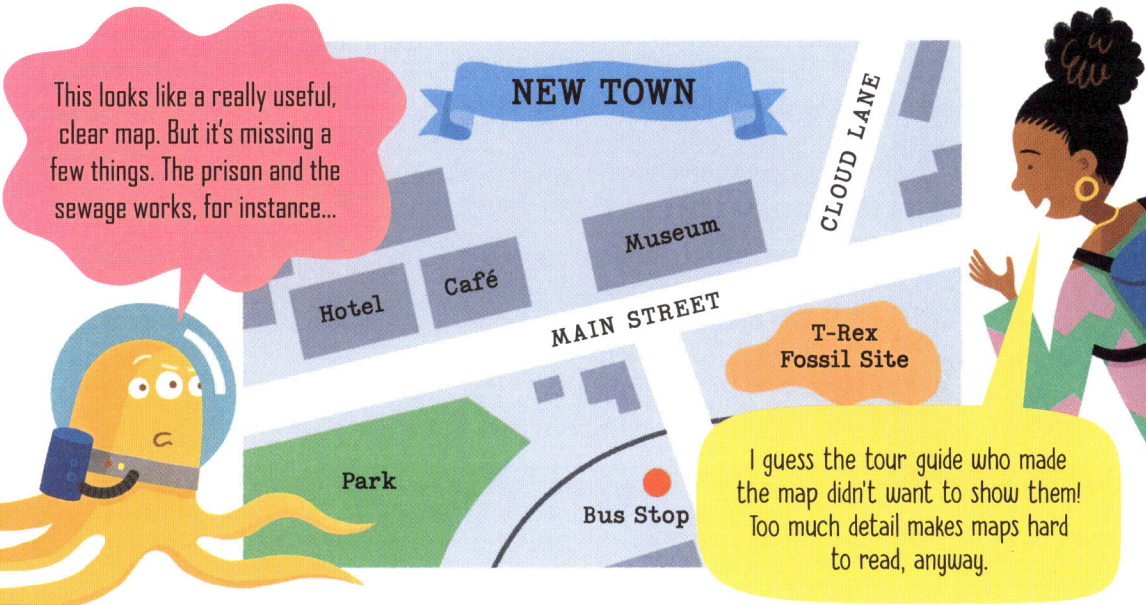

One purpose of a map is to pinpoint places precisely, so it's easy to find them again. To achieve this, some maps are divided into horizontal lines – known as lines of **latitude** – and vertical lines, know as lines of **longitude**. Any place can be described by the intersection of these lines – also known as its **coordinates**.

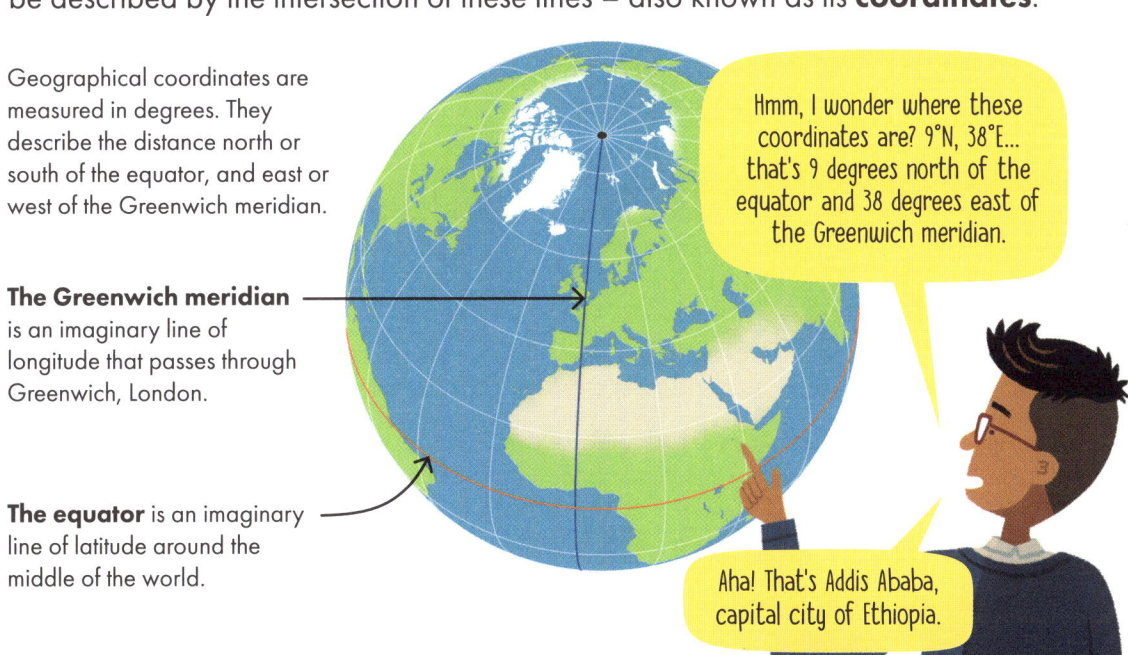

Overlapping data

Geographers find it useful to combine and study different kinds of data, and show it on a map. They use a kind of technology known as geographic information systems (GIS).

Using GIS, geographers can overlap data about housing, climate change, flooding, satellite imagery – whatever it is they want to explore – and show it on a single map.

Landforms

Housing

Flooding

Base map

On a GIS map, it's easier to spot links and patterns from seemingly unrelated data.

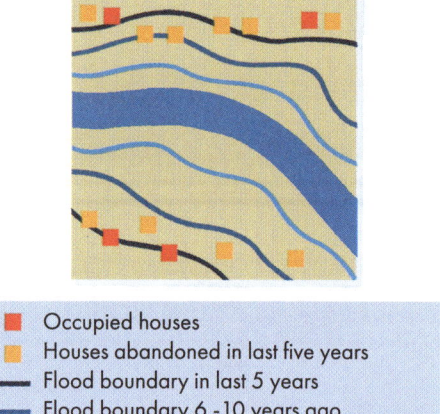

- Occupied houses
- Houses abandoned in last five years
- Flood boundary in last 5 years
- Flood boundary 6-10 years ago
- Flood boundary 11-15 years ago

A GIS map might show a link between people moving away and flash floods in an area, for example. Research might show that bigger, more frequent floods are driving people away from previously desirable homes by a river.

People use GIS more than you think. It's used in navigation systems in cars and on maps and other apps.

How will you find your way to the waterfall?

I have a GIS map on my phone that combines satellite data with a map of the area showing local landmarks.

Can you find a quick route that also has a nice café halfway there?

Yes, when I type café into the search bar, the map shows all the cafés in the area. I can also check traffic information to find the quickest route. Thank goodness for GIS.

GIS has been particularly effective at identifying links between issues such as health and the environment, transforming the treatment of numerous diseases across the world.

I'm using GIS to study how a disease spread in this town. Looks as if it started... here.

This idea stems from a ground-breaking discovery by British doctor, John Snow. In 1854, long before computers existed, Dr. Snow combined a map with other data to investigate an outbreak of a disease in London called cholera.

Cholera was a deadly disease. In the early 19th century, most doctors thought it spread through air...

...but Dr. Snow had a theory that it spread through water. And he had an idea about how to prove it.

During a cholera outbreak in Soho, London, Snow plotted cholera cases and water pumps together on a map.

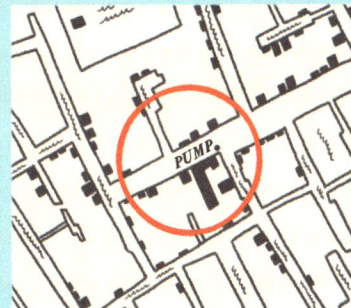

Snow's map instantly showed that the biggest cluster of cholera cases was close to one particular pump.

When the pump's handle was removed, the cholera outbreak in Soho immediately stopped.

Snow's map proved that cholera was *caused by dirty water. This discovery has since saved countless lives.*

CHAPTER 1
Journey into the Earth

A lot of what's on Earth is shaped by what's going on INSIDE it – from volcanic eruptions to the height of mountains, to how some animals find their way on long journeys.

Exploring the insides of Earth isn't easy though. So geographers rely on clues, such as rocks and tremors, to create a picture of what's going on. Read on to find out what they know about the Earth, how they know it, and what experts are still trying to find out...

How do we know...
...what happened so long ago?

By looking at these kinds of clues.

Moving plates

The Earth's surface is made up of sections called **tectonic plates** that slowly move.

This has caused many changes on the Earth's surface, such as continents drifting apart over millions of years.

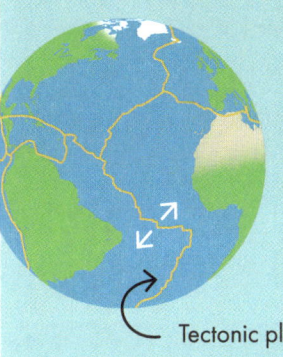

Tectonic plate boundary

Ice

Ice sheets are made from layers of snowfall that go back hundreds of thousands of years.

Drilling long chunks out of the ice sheet allows us to look at these different layers.

Scientists can work out what air used to be made up of, by examining air bubbles trapped inside the ice.

Rocks

Rocks are so old and last so long that they help tell Earth's early history.

This kind of rock is created by underwater volcanic eruption. So we know water has been on Earth at least as long as this rock.

3.8 billion-years-old pillow lava

Fossils

Buried inside rocks, you can sometimes see the shapes of animals and plants that lived millions of years ago. These are known as **fossils**.

We know some areas of land used to be under the sea, because of all the fossils of sea creatures discovered in the rocks.

Look inside the Earth

If you *could* cut into the Earth, you'd find different layers, each one hotter than the last. Here's geographers' best guess at how those layers work.

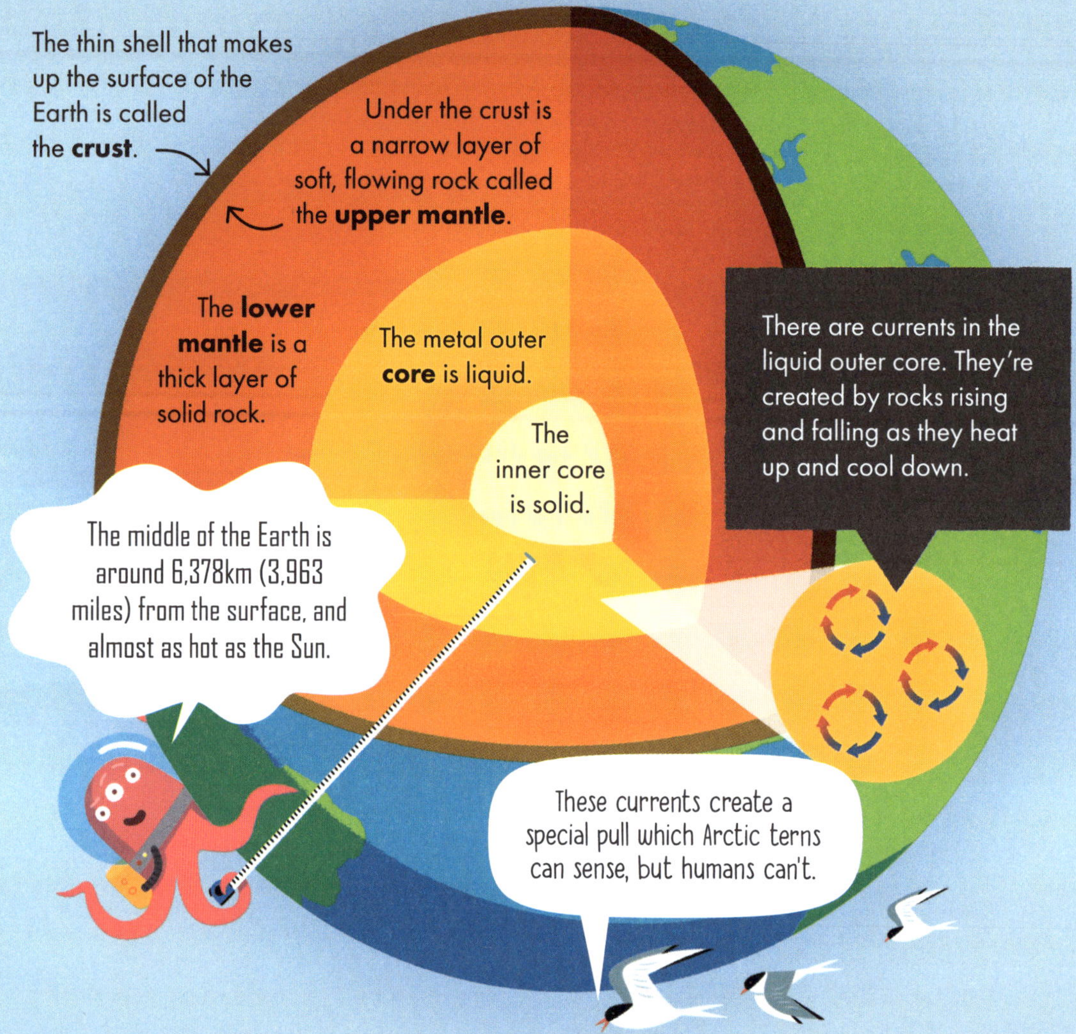

The thin shell that makes up the surface of the Earth is called the **crust**.

Under the crust is a narrow layer of soft, flowing rock called the **upper mantle**.

The **lower mantle** is a thick layer of solid rock.

The metal outer **core** is liquid.

The inner core is solid.

There are currents in the liquid outer core. They're created by rocks rising and falling as they heat up and cool down.

The middle of the Earth is around 6,378km (3,963 miles) from the surface, and almost as hot as the Sun.

These currents create a special pull which Arctic terns can sense, but humans can't.

The currents in the outer core make the Earth magnetic. Scientists don't totally understand how it works, but it's to do with the way the currents generate electricity.

This means magnetic objects are attracted to or repelled by the ends of the Earth, known as its **magnetic poles**. That's why the needle on a compass points North. Birds sense this pull too, and it helps them navigate on long journeys.

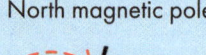
North magnetic pole

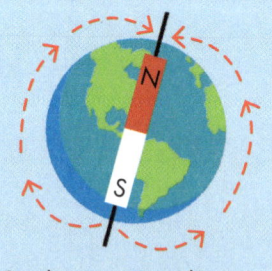
South magnetic pole

The furthest we've ever dug into the Earth is a 12.2km (7.6 mile) deep borehole that took 22 years to drill. But this is only about a third of the way through the crust.

It's impossible to *see* inside the Earth. Instead, geographers rely on *listening* to what's going on inside, using special instruments.

The best time to listen is when the Earth shakes during an **earthquake**. A machine called a **seismometer** records the shock waves that travel through the Earth.

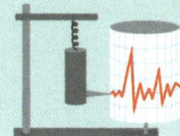

Scientists know that the waves change speed and direction as they go through different materials.

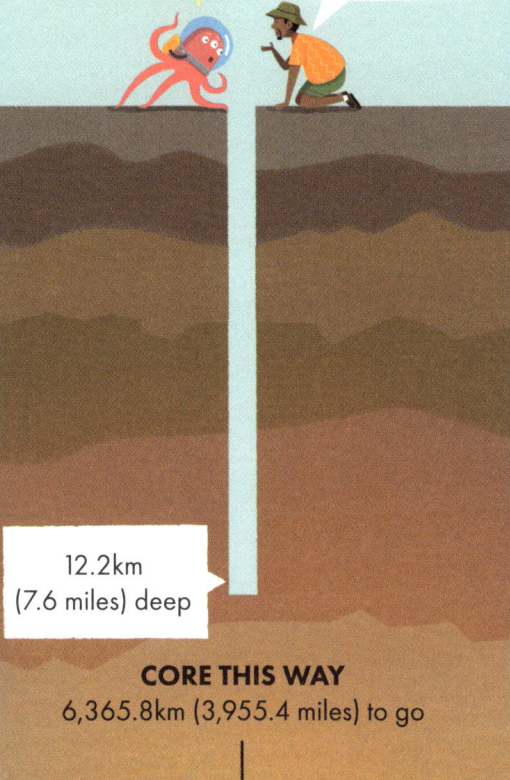

Kola Superdeep Borehole, Russia

What's it like down there?

It's very rocky and twice as hot as scientists expected. That's why they had to stop drilling.

12.2km (7.6 miles) deep

CORE THIS WAY
6,365.8km (3,955.4 miles) to go
↓

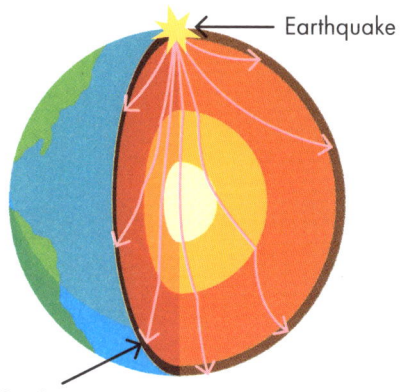

Earthquake

Shock waves

This allows them to work out what the different layers are made of and whether they are solid or liquid.

You don't seem to know much about the inside of your planet.

Indeed not. We do make educated guesses. But, as the Superdeep Borehole showed, they're not always correct. There's still MUCH to discover.

A moving jigsaw puzzle

The Earth's crust and upper mantle are made up of huge rocky pieces called **tectonic plates**. The plates float slowly on currents of flowing rock below. This constant movement causes big natural features, such as mountain ranges or ocean trenches, to build up over time.

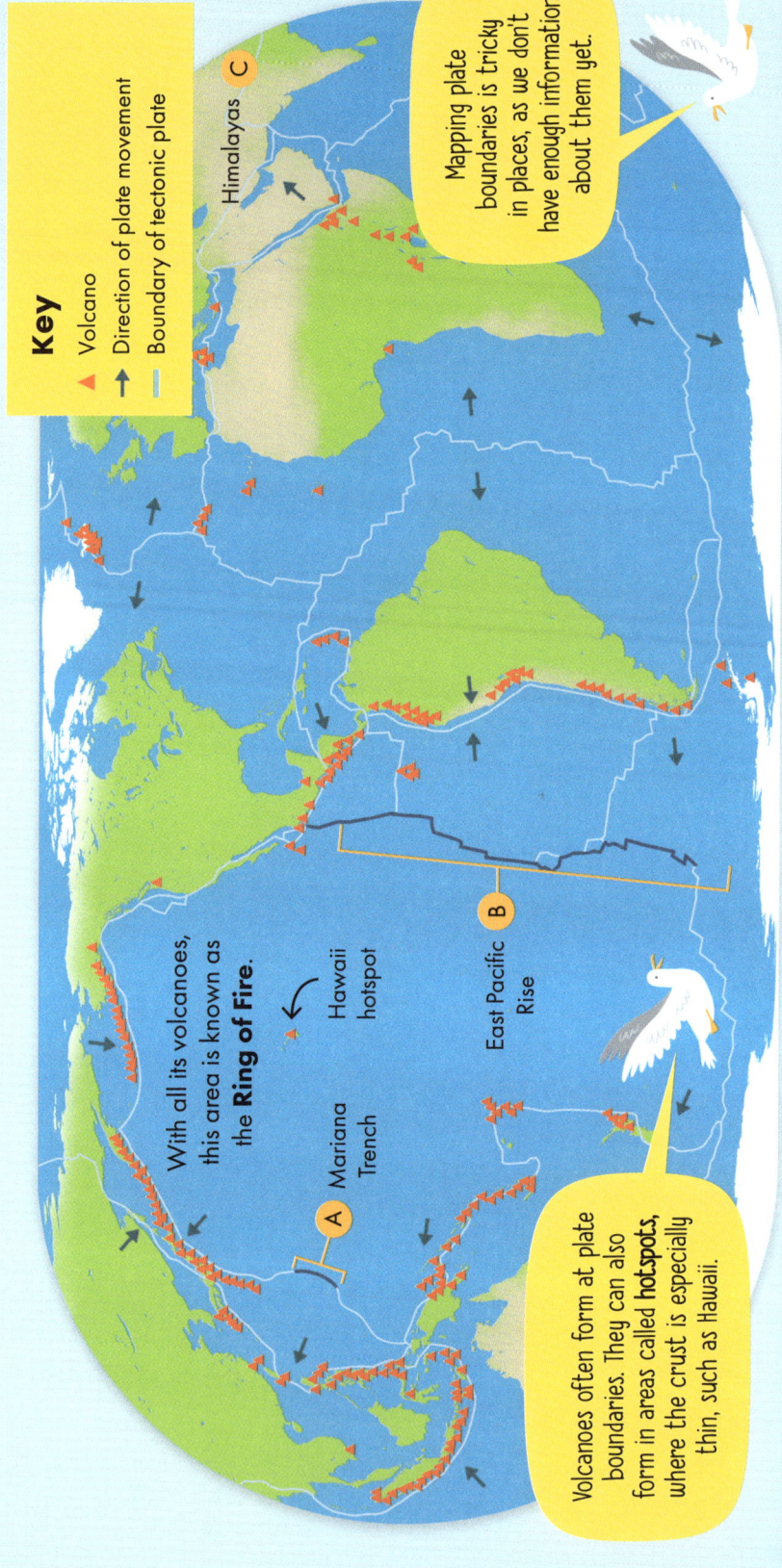

Mountains

When land on either side of two plates is PUSHED together, the crust can be forced up to form big mountains.

C This is happening in the Himalayan mountains, which are still growing.

Volcanic eruptions

A volcanic eruption is when **magma** bursts out through a crack in the Earth's crust. Eruptions usually occur near the edges of tectonic plates, by ridges or trenches.

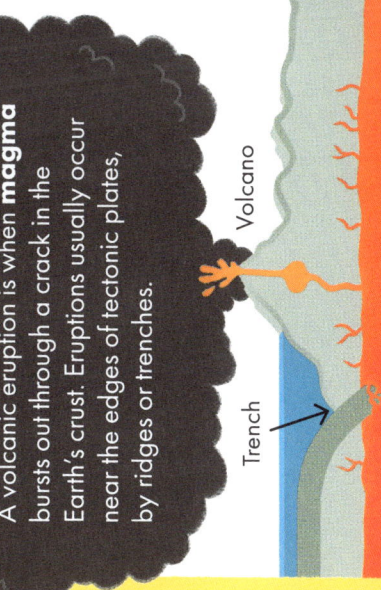

The rocks in the bottom plate melt, and rise up through cracks.

Ridges

When plates on the ocean floor move apart, hot flowing rock below called **magma** rises, then cools, forming new crust.

This is a kind of volcano.

B The East Pacific Rise is spreading apart the fastest. It moves 16cm (6.3in) further apart every year.

Tsunamis

When an earthquake or erupting volcano shifts a lot of water under the sea, it can send pulses of water surging through the sea.

As they reach shallow water near a coast, the pulses bunch up and grow into giant waves called **tsunamis**.

Trenches

When plates in the ocean push together, one plate sinks and forms an ocean trench.

A The bottom of the Mariana Trench is about 11km (7 miles) below sea level. It's the deepest trench in the world.

Earthquakes

When plates in the sea or on land slide against each other, they can catch and become jammed.

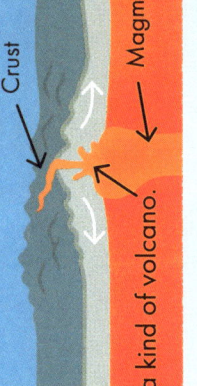

Eventually the rocks give way, and the shock sends vibrations through the crust. This is called an **earthquake**.

Living with volcanoes

The land around you shapes every aspect of your life – especially when you live in the shadow of a deadly, active volcano, such as Nyiragongo, in the Democratic Republic of Congo.

During eruptions, clouds of ash destroy crops. But over time the ash breaks down and enriches the soil, making it easy to grow lots of food.

Nyiragongo

The rich soil also produces jungles that teem with life. A third of all mountain gorillas around the world live here, and feast on the many different plants.

The rocks are full of rare, expensive metals, brought near to the surface by past eruptions. But the people who mine them are often working in terrible conditions. Armed groups sometimes fight to control the mines, as metals such as copper and cobalt can be sold for a *lot* of money.

Munch

A national park attracts visitors and creates jobs.

Munch

The mines should be a source of wealth for us, but at the moment that's not the case.

Many of the buildings in town were rebuilt after recent eruptions. My job is to monitor the volcano, so we have enough time to leave before the *next* eruption.

We say the volcano has two faces. It kills...

...and it brings us life.

22

Expedition volcano

At the Goma volcano observatory we monitor Nyiragongo minute by minute, to help us work out when it might erupt. These are the kinds of things we look out for.

Aurore Ndjoko, volcano expert

GROUND MOVEMENT

We use machines to track the movement of the ground, and record it on graphs like these.

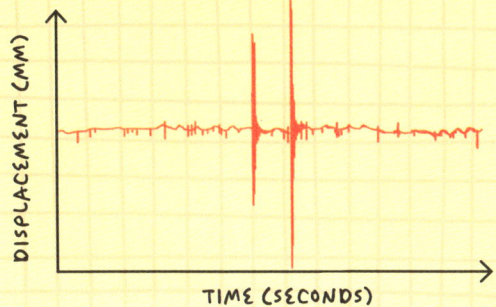

LAVA SOUNDS

There's some information we can only get by visiting the volcano itself...

...and sometimes even abseiling down into the crater.

This is me going down to install microphones around the crater. They pick up sounds the lava makes as it rises and falls.

GAS

Planes can gather air samples to see how much gas and ash is spewing out of the volcano. An increase in gas and ash suggests an eruption is likely.

ROCKS

We collect rocks that have been ejected out of the volcano. They're made of lava that's cooled and set. Their structure tells us how liquid the lava was and how quickly it might spread during an eruption.

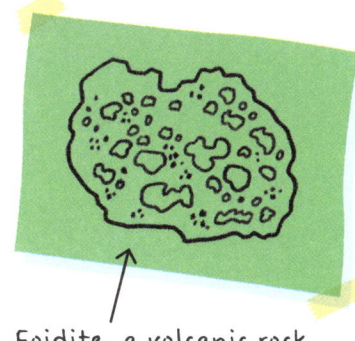

Foidite, a volcanic rock

Every rock has a story

Types of geographers known as **geologists** study what rocks are made of in order to help explain the world around us. From space travel to giant natural sculptures – here are some of the stories rocks can tell.

Every day, rocks known as **meteorites** fall to Earth from space. They're full of clues about what planets, asteroids and comets are made of.

Many rocks were formed millions of years ago. What's in them, and where they are, can tell us about the past.

Scientists look for cracks in rock, and measure tremors, to calculate where and when an earthquake might happen.

Many rocks on Earth's surface are sculpted by rain, wind, ice, rivers, seas and temperature changes. The results can be so spectacular, people tell magical stories to explain them.

According to *legend*, the Giant's Causeway in Ireland is what's left of a bridge that giants built between Ireland and Scotland.

According to *geographers*, lava erupted through cracks here 50 million years ago, and cooled to form hexagonal columns. Waves slowly wore away the tops.

The bigger picture

There's lots to learn from looking at the rocks in a whole landscape, too. Rocks are constantly changing and being recycled into new rocks – in a process that takes millions of years. It's known as... the **rock cycle**.

When hot molten rock from the Earth's interior cools down, it forms rocks known as **igneous rocks**.

Wow! It's as if the Earth itself is a living thing.

Over time, wind, water, ice and heat break down rocks on the surface.

Smaller pieces of rock then get carried away and end up at the bottom of lakes and seas.

Some rocks get dragged underground or squished upwards into mountains by moving tectonic plates. Extreme heat and pressure turns them into new kinds of rocks, known as **metamorphic rocks**.

Fragments of rock, plant and animal matter build up in layers, and turn into **sedimentary rocks** over time.

Every rock on Earth fits somewhere into this cycle.

Earth power

Enormous quantities of underground materials are dug up each year to generate energy for electricity, fuel and heating.

Coal, oil and gas

These are all formed over millions of years from bits of plants and animals buried under the ground. They're known as **fossil fuels**.

Oil is turned into fuel and burned to power cars, buses, trains, planes, ships...

Gas is used for heating water and buildings and for cooking.

Coal and gas can be burned in **power stations** to generate electricity.

All these fossil fuels are relatively cheap and easy to make energy from.

But they take millions of years to form and we may run out.

Also, burning fossil fuels releases polluting gases. This is a big cause of rising global temperatures known as **climate change**.

Uranium

Uranium is a **radioactive** metal, which means it naturally wants to break apart. When this happens it releases lots of heat, and is known as **nuclear fission**.

Nuclear power stations use nuclear fission to generate electricity.

Nuclear fuel produced this way is very efficient. One kilogram (2lb) of uranium can generate 20,000 times more energy than the same amount of coal.

It doesn't release warming gases.

But it does create dangerous nuclear waste, which has to be kept safe in carefully sealed containers for *many* years.

DO NOT TOUCH FOR 1,000 YEARS

Look, I know you love rocks. But there are LOTS of ways of generating energy without burning fossil fuels. For example, by using energy from the sun and wind.

You're right, but those methods DO still involve rocks! Turn the page to see what I mean.

Relying on rocks

Shifting away from relying on fossil fuels is a big part of tackling climate change. But converting the energy of the Sun and wind to make **clean electricity** still involves rocks...

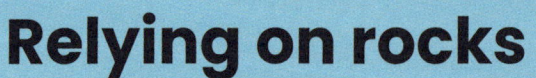

Wind turbines use the wind's movement to turn a turbine and generate electricity. Most of the turbine is made of materials that come from rocks. These include steel (made from iron and carbon), plastic and a variety of metals.

Solar panels convert light from the Sun into electricity. The energy has to be stored in batteries, made of materials such as lithium, cobalt and nickel which come from inside the Earth.

Modern technology

The things people often want – better hospitals, more houses, fast trains, modern technology – traditionally require using *more and more* resources and energy. But we have limited supplies of both fossil fuels and the materials used in clean energy.

So the challenge is: can we keep doing *more* with *less*?

Well, we've got to get better at reusing materials rather than throwing them away.

And we need to invent more efficient ways of doing things. For example, these new bricks were made using very little energy. Instead of being fired in an oven, they were injected with some hardening bacteria.

Rocky relationships

The way people think about the Earth and the materials it holds depends a lot on where and how they live, and which problems they're most worried about. It's easy to ignore rocks, and think they're just the stuff we walk on. But ultimately, they shape ALL our lives, and our future too.

In our town, EVERYONE earns a living by working for the nearby mine, or by supporting the people who work there.

Everyday life is possible thanks to all the energy and materials we extract from the Earth. But I worry about the environmental impact a lot.

TOWN · MINE · CITY

My tribe's ancestors have been meeting here for over 45,000 years. What right do mining companies have to come and blow up our caves?

We're researching a way to make steel that doesn't involve burning loads of coal. If we succeed, it will be a big help in tackling climate change.

POWER STATION

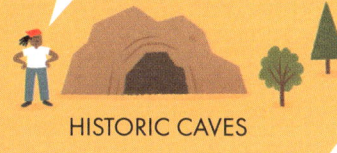

HISTORIC CAVES

NEW MINE PROJECT

UNIVERSITY

We're looking for new sources of useful earth materials. If we can't keep up with demand, everything around the world will get more expensive.

OCEAN BORDER

We use four times fewer resources than the people in the rich country over the sea. They should close THEIR mines and oil rigs, and learn to manage with less.

OIL RIG

OIL RIG

CHAPTER 2
Weather and climate

Our planet is surrounded by a swirling layer of gases called the **atmosphere**. The day-to-day changes in the atmosphere are known as the **weather** – and a whole branch of geography known as **meteorology** is dedicated to studying it.

Other geographers focus on the bigger picture – how the Earth's weather has changed over the last few decades or even centuries. This is the study of the **climate** and the people who study it are called **climate geographers**.

Climate geographers were among the first to notice that the Earth's climate has been changing more quickly over the last century than ever before.

> Let's start with a tour of the atmosphere. I know it well from my journey down to Earth.

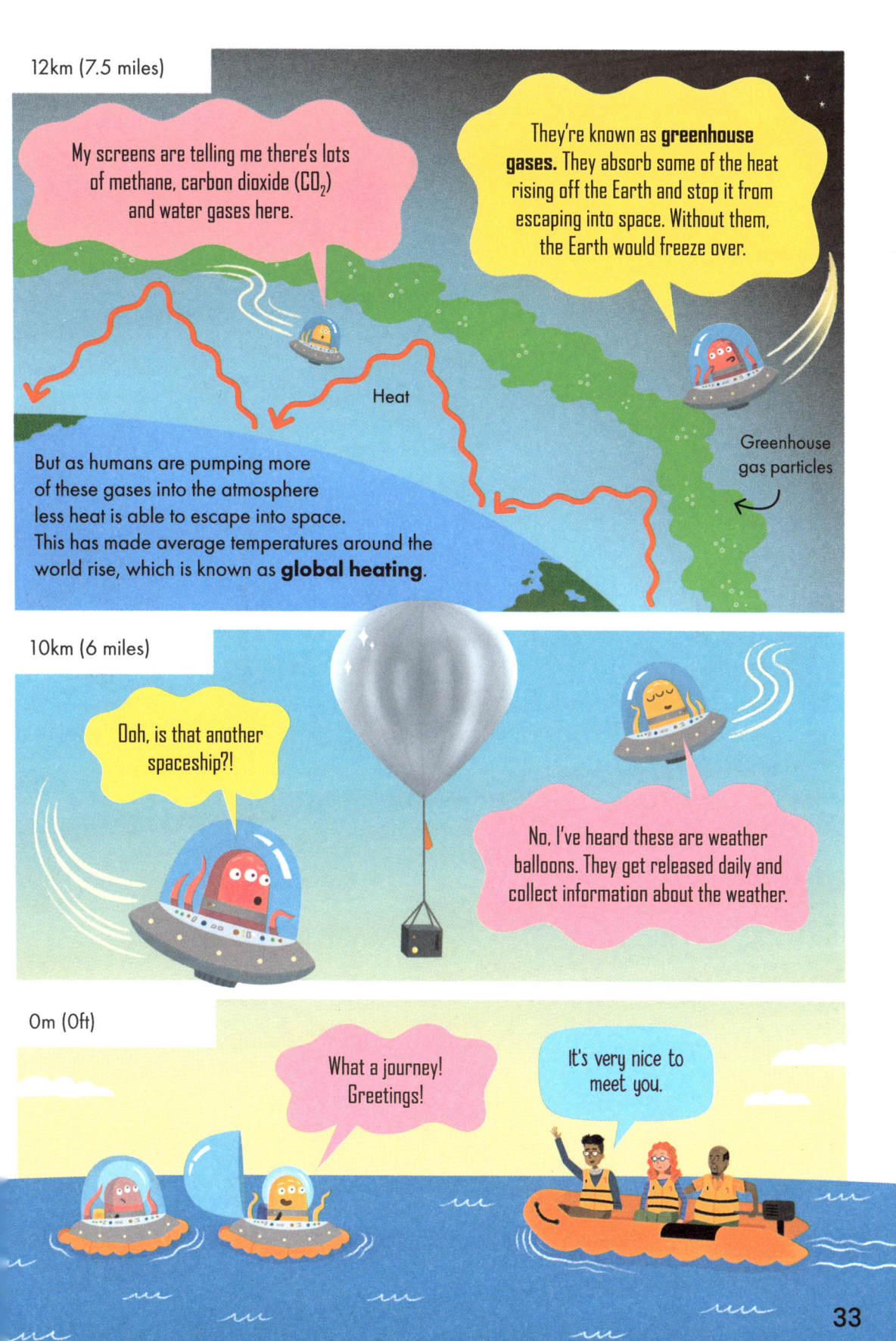

What's up with the weather?

Most people pay attention to the weather – whether they're choosing what to wear, harvesting crops or flying a plane. But looking out of the window will only tell you so much. You really need a *lot* of data, powerful computers and teams working together to make sense of it completely.

Every minute of the day, weather data is collected...

Wind strength | Cloud cover | Humidity | Rainfall | Temperature | Air pressure – the amount of air particles in the air

...from over 10,000 sources around the world.

Aircraft | Weather balloons | Weather radar | Automated weather stations | Weather satellites

The data is shared with weather forecasting agencies. They use computers to compare the data with past weather patterns, in order to predict the weather in the near future.

But even with loads of data and powerful computers, it's very hard to make accurate forecasts more than two weeks ahead. This is because the most miniscule change in the atmosphere can have a big impact on future weather conditions.

A tiny difference in weather conditions today, such as the location of a single cloud...

...can lead to very different weather two weeks later.

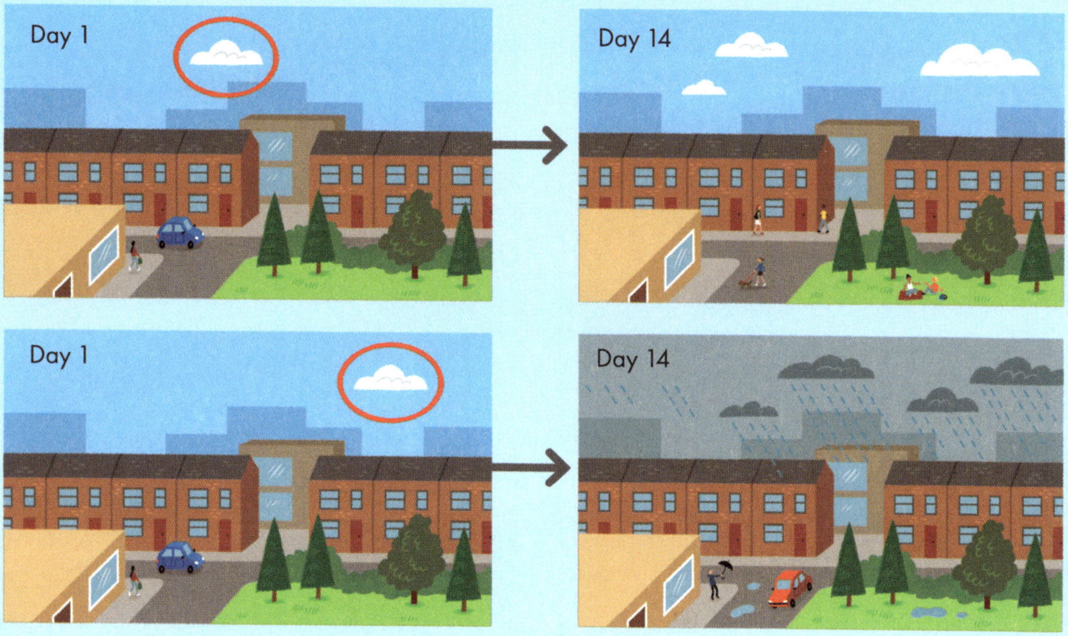

Butterfly effect

This idea, that tiny changes can have large consequences, came to be known as the **butterfly effect**. It was discovered in the 1960s, after weather expert Edward Lorenz suggested that a butterfly flapping its wings in Brazil might trigger (or prevent) a giant wind storm forming over Texas.

You can't ACTUALLY create a storm by using specially trained butterflies. But the flap of wings does have enough impact to change the outcome of the weather.

This idea has been applied to lots of other areas of geography where tiny changes can make a big difference. For example, it helps explain how a very small rise in sea temperature could wipe out many species of sea creatures.

35

Extreme weather

Extreme weather is when there is a big disruption to usual weather patterns, that puts people and wildlife in danger. This includes long periods without rain known as **droughts**, dramatic spinning winds known as **tornadoes**, or giant storms known as **hurricanes**.

1. Hurricanes develop in late summer, when seas are at their warmest. Damp air spirals up and forms thunderclouds as it cools.

Hurricane seen from space

2. Winds twist the clouds together into a single spinning storm. When they reach speeds of over 119km/h (74mph) the storm is classified as a hurricane.

3. Once the hurricane reaches land, strong winds, torrential rain and high tides can cause severe damage and flooding.

Depending on where they start in the world, hurricanes are also known as cyclones or typhoons – and in northern Australia as willy-willies.

Often well over 380km (240 miles) wide

In May 2008, *Cyclone Nargis* battered the coast of Myanmar. It turned into the country's worst ever natural disaster for a variety of reasons...

The hardest hit area, the Irrawaddy Delta, is densely populated and only just above sea level.

There was no emergency evacuation plan in place, despite powerful storms hitting Myanmar every one or two years.

May, 2009
Remembering Cyclone Nargis

- 140,000 people dead
- Up to 2.5 million homeless
- 40% of food stores destroyed

The government initially refused help from other countries.

Almost 70% of the population lost access to clean drinking water.

Many mangrove forests, which protect the coast from flooding, had previously been chopped down to make room for farming.

Maps save lives

The solution to defend against extreme weather is making an accurate forecast that gives people enough time to get out of the way. Maps using GIS, such as this hurricane forecast one, can help people understand the risks and plan ahead.

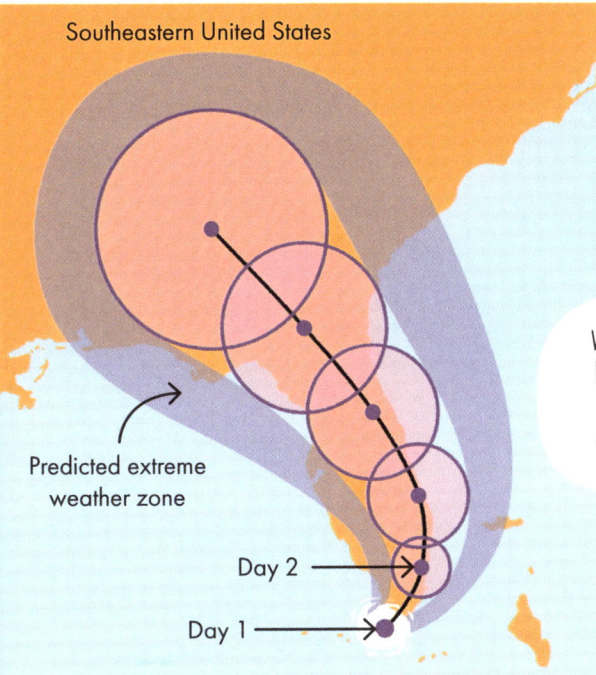

This is known as a **cone of uncertainty graph**. The pale pink cone is the area the hurricane *could* travel through over six days, based on the predictions of lots of different organizations.

We live right on the black line. We've packed up and are going to a shelter outside the danger zone.

But many people read these kinds of maps incorrectly, and this has real life and death consequences.

It looks like the hurricane gets bigger and bigger from its starting point. I live at the thin end, so I don't need to evacuate.

I don't live on the black line, so I'm probably safe.

The size of the cone has nothing to do with the size of the hurricane. Over time there is more and more uncertainty about where the hurricane might head, so the area it might travel through gets wider.

This black line follows the forecast of the hurricane division of the US National Weather Service. But the hurricane might take any path inside the cone, or even one *outside* the cone (a one in three chance).

Geographers are always looking for ways to make their maps clear and easy to follow. But it's a challenge!

What's up with the climate?

Every place has *days* of extreme weather, but the climate is the pattern of weather *over a year*. The simplest way to study it is to look at temperature and rainfall on graphs, such as the ones below.

Riyadh, in Saudi Arabia, has long sweltering summers, and mild dry winters. It's a **hot desert climate**.

Hanoi, in Vietnam, has hot, wet summers, and warm, dryer winters. It's a **tropical climate**.

■ Rainfall ● Temperature

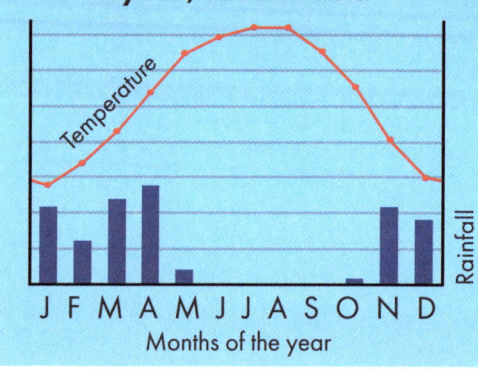

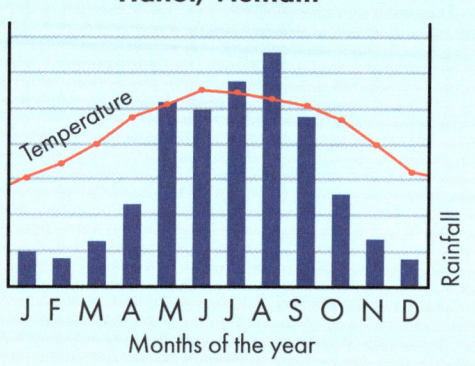

A place's climate is usually shaped by:

Sunlight
Sunlight has the biggest impact. Regions closer to the equator get more light and heat from the Sun, while those further away are colder and darker.

Wind
Winds can make places colder or warmer, wetter or dryer depending on where they've blown in from.

Altitude
Hills and mountains force air to rise up, making it cooler.

Sea
Regions near the sea tend to be more humid, as the air is full of moisture.

Climate change

Changes in the climate over thousands of years are normal. But when people talk about **climate change**, they're usually referring to the rapid changes from recent decades caused by us.

As we burn fossil fuels, and cut down trees, the amount of CO_2 (and other greenhouse gases) in the atmosphere increases. This accelerates global heating.

As temperatures creep up, especially at the poles, they trigger natural processes which make the Earth EVEN hotter.

1. Ice is white, so it's good at reflecting heat. As icy areas at the poles shrink...

2. ...less heat is reflected, and more is ABSORBED by the darker sea and land.

3. So the Earth gets hotter, and more ice melts... and so on.

As well as *collecting* data that shows the Earth is warming up, it's also up to geographers to *share* it so that people know what's happening. American geographer Joan Sheldon knitted a scarf, as a way to describe global heating.

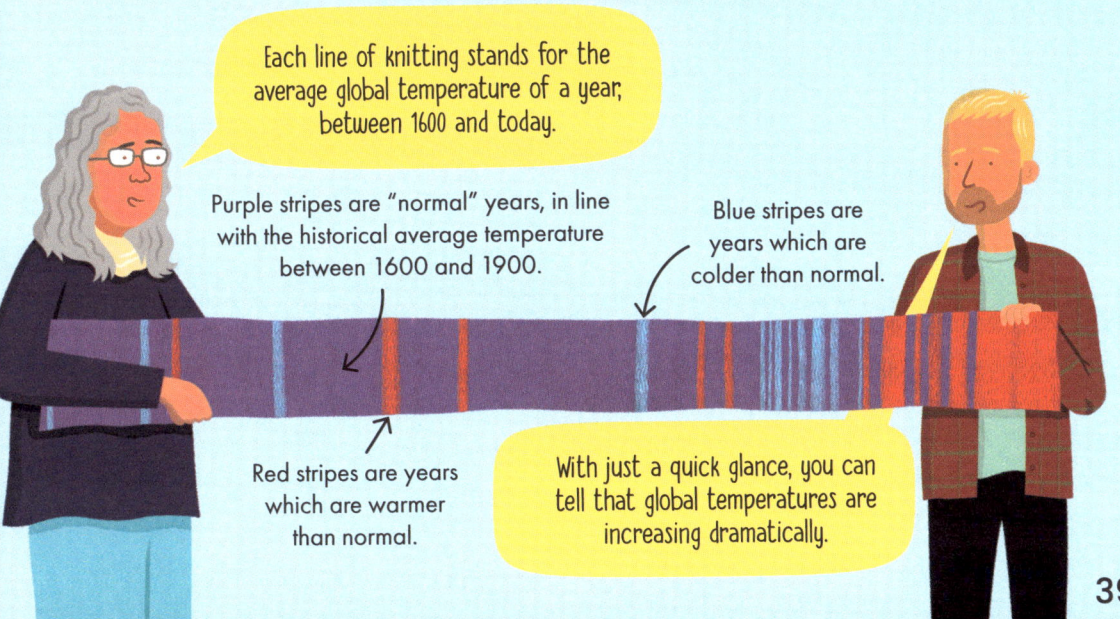

Each line of knitting stands for the average global temperature of a year, between 1600 and today.

Purple stripes are "normal" years, in line with the historical average temperature between 1600 and 1900.

Blue stripes are years which are colder than normal.

Red stripes are years which are warmer than normal.

With just a quick glance, you can tell that global temperatures are increasing dramatically.

39

Just a few degrees

Lately, average global temperatures have risen by a few degrees. It sounds small, but it's having an impact everywhere. Here are some of the changes geographers have found that are happening already.

Northern Europe — Wet areas are getting wetter, as warm air holds more water.

Arctic Ocean — Animal homes are under threat – especially in icy places which are heating up the fastest.

Japan — Melting ice leads to rising sea levels, which is bad news for low-lying coastal cities.

The Sahel — Dry areas are getting dryer. Hotter and erratic weather makes it harder to grow food and reduces the supply of water – especially in dry places.

India — There's a higher chance of extreme weather events – especially in warmer parts of the world.

Pacific Ocean

Climate change affects places in different ways. Cooler, richer places are likely to be less impacted than hotter, poorer ones.

I already struggle with droughts, but now they're getting worse.

Some geographers investigate not just what changes are happening, but how different parts of the world are causing them. For example, here's how different regions have contributed to global CO_2 emissions since the 1750s.

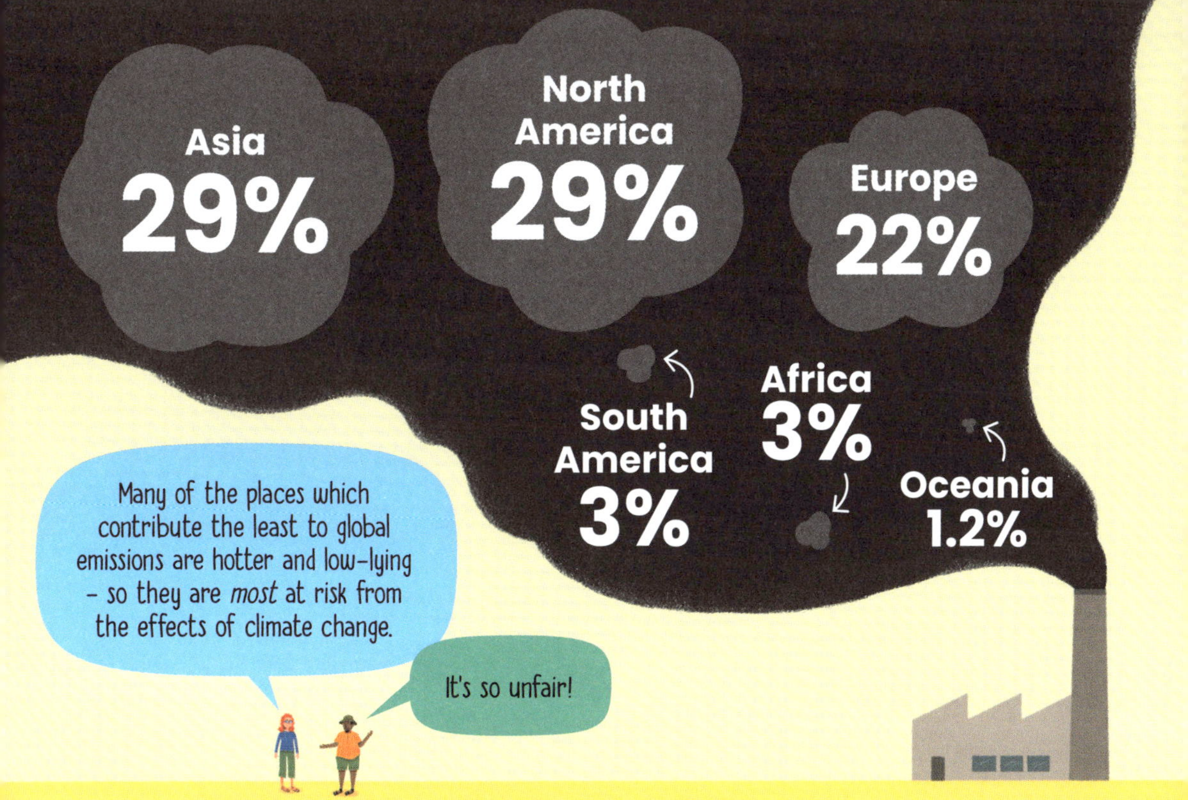

Asia 29%

North America 29%

Europe 22%

South America 3%

Africa 3%

Oceania 1.2%

Many of the places which contribute the least to global emissions are hotter and low-lying – so they are *most* at risk from the effects of climate change.

It's so unfair!

Making sense of the causes and consequences of global heating is a big part of geography. Some geographers also investigate possible solutions, such as these:

I'm working to make my city net zero by 2050. That means finding ways for the city to produce as much carbon-free energy as its inhabitants need.

Zero Carbon Team Lead

Powered by RENEWABLE ENERGY

My job is to find ways to protect coasts from flooding and erosion due to rising sea levels. for example, here I recommended building a sea wall.

Across the world, people are finding clever ways to help!

Coastal conservationist

Biomes

The climate has a big impact on landscapes, animals and plants. Taken together, these form something geographers call a **biome**. There are many different biomes, but they occur in several parts of the world. Geographers often use maps to show where they appear.

Central and South America

Sonoran Desert

Tropical rainforest – thrives in the hot, wet climate, home to more animal and plant species than anywhere on Earth. Sometimes called *the lungs of the Earth*, rainforests draw in CO_2 and breathe out oxygen.

Amazon Rainforest

Cerrado grasslands

Major types of biomes

Desert – very dry, and extremely hot or cold depending on latitude, very little can survive

Mediterranean – shrubland with a warm, dry summer and mild winter

Mountain – cold, icy and with little life higher up, but warmer, with forests and meadows lower down

Andes mountains

Tropical grassland – fertile grasslands with cool winters and warm summers

Temperate forest – forested areas with cold winters and warm summers

Temperate grassland – warm grasslands with a dry season, followed by a rainy season

What about people?

Maps of biomes, such as the one to the left, often don't show people. This helps keep visuals clear and simple. But human activity shapes every biome, too.

Farming often has the biggest direct impact on natural landscapes.

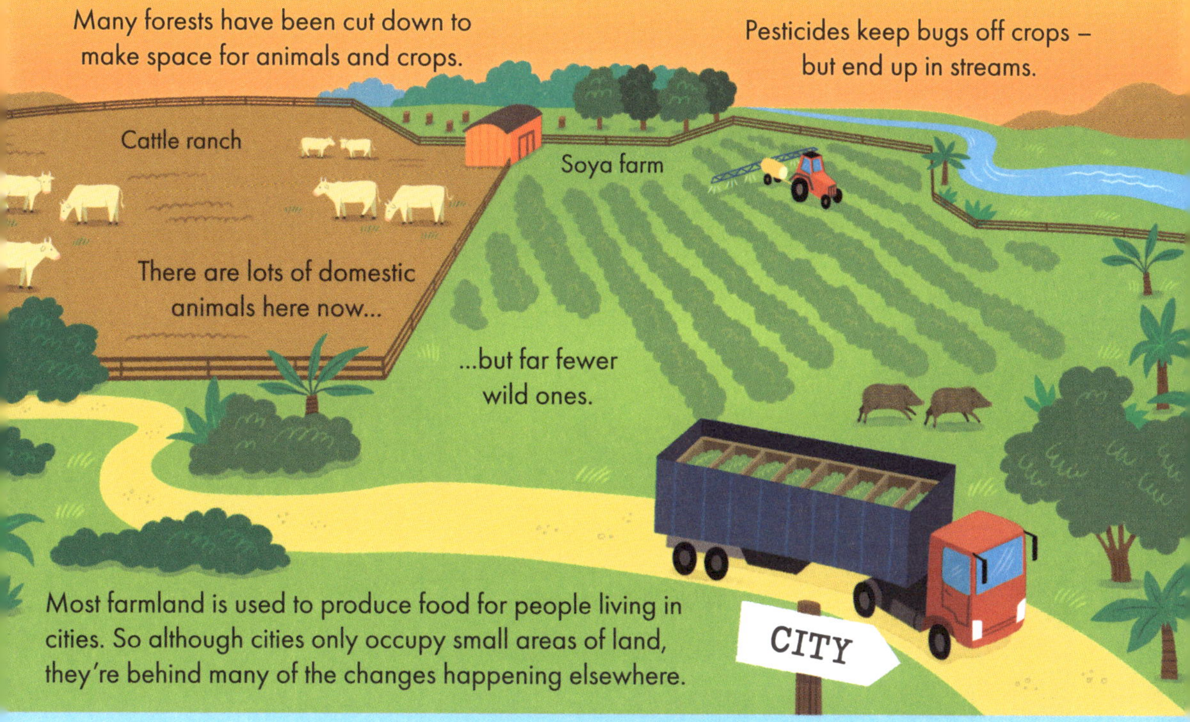

Many forests have been cut down to make space for animals and crops.

Pesticides keep bugs off crops – but end up in streams.

Cattle ranch

Soya farm

There are lots of domestic animals here now...

...but far fewer wild ones.

Most farmland is used to produce food for people living in cities. So although cities only occupy small areas of land, they're behind many of the changes happening elsewhere.

In some places, people have managed to live within a landscape for centuries, without changing it very much. They tend to be **indigenous people** – people who have lived there for hundreds and hundreds of years, and have a special relationship with the land.

"Our family has lived in the Amazon rainforest for centuries. We hunt and gather food to eat, and try to keep logging companies off our land."

Geographers have a lot to learn from people with such a strong connection to nature. Research has shown that indigenous people of the Amazon are more successful at safeguarding their rainforest home than government or charity projects.

CHAPTER 3
Watery world

For billions of people, water is perhaps the most vital resource of all. We need it to drink, to grow crops, as a home for fish, for washing, and for making energy and all sorts of products, including paper and steel.

One thing geographers are exploring is how humans can use water in such a way that will ensure there is enough for everyone now AND for future generations.

I can see why Earth is known as the Blue Planet.

Blue planet

Seen from Space, planet Earth is mostly blue – that's because more than 70% of its surface is covered in water.

I've never seen such a watery planet.

Those wispy white bits are water too – clouds, apparently.

About 97.5% of all Earth's water is found in its seas and oceans. This water is salty and has other rock minerals dissolved in it as well.

The remaining 2.5% is fresh water. This is the water that we use every day – for drinking and cleaning and making things.

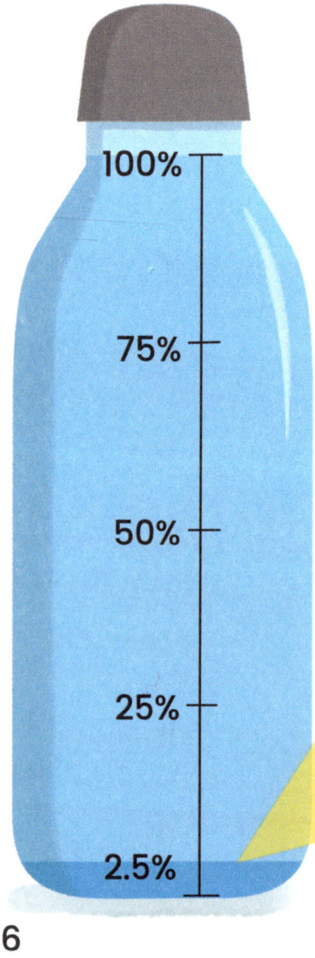

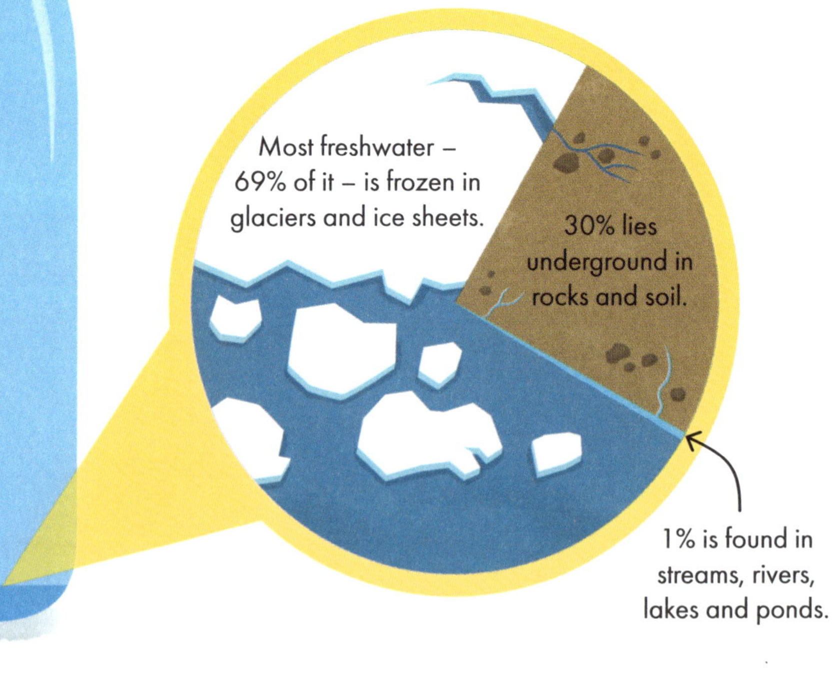

Most freshwater – 69% of it – is frozen in glaciers and ice sheets.

30% lies underground in rocks and soil.

1% is found in streams, rivers, lakes and ponds.

Amazingly, all this water is connected. It constantly moves from one place to another, through a process known as the **water cycle**.

2. Droplets of water in clouds grow larger and heavier, eventually falling as rain, snow, sleet or hail.

1. The Sun's heat turns surface water into a gas that rises then cools to form clouds of water droplets.

3. Water frozen in icy glaciers and snowy mountain peaks gradually melts and flows downhill.

4. The water runs into streams and rivers.

5. Eventually water reaches lakes and oceans.

Some water seeps into the soil and through layers of rock deeper in the ground.

The water cycle continues endlessly, which means we're drinking the same water people have always drunk. In fact, it's the same water dinosaurs drank!

Certain things can alter the way water cycles around.

For example, in order to store water, people sometimes block rivers to form artificial lakes known as **reservoirs**. This drastically reshapes the landscape.

47

Seas and oceans

Earth's oceans are all connected. Typically, geographers divide one globe-spanning ocean into a few separate ones, such as the Pacific and Atlantic. This page shows a map of the world putting the oceans in the middle. It was designed by Dr. Athelstan Spilhaus and shows how central these vast waters are to our world.

Sea water is constantly moving in currents of warmer and colder water. This affects the climate and weather, and the movement of animals.

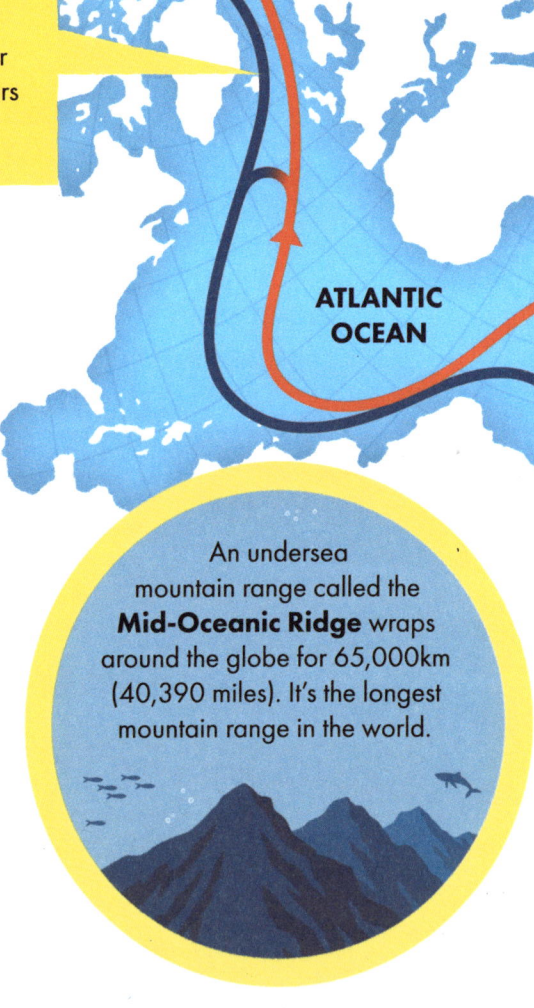

ARCTIC OCEAN

ATLANTIC OCEAN

These lines represent a system of currents called the **global conveyor belt**. Warmer currents are shown in red; colder currents in blue. It takes water 1,000 years to complete a single circuit.

At least half the oxygen we need is made by microscopic plants and algae floating in the ocean. So, every breath we take connects us to the world's seas and oceans.

An undersea mountain range called the **Mid-Oceanic Ridge** wraps around the globe for 65,000km (40,390 miles). It's the longest mountain range in the world.

A defrosting planet

One thing geographers have been measuring is sea and land-ice loss due to rising temperatures – and the effects this will have on sea levels.

During the winter, most of the Arctic is covered in sea ice. In the warmer summer months, much of the ice melts. However, rising temperatures are causing the area covered by ice in summer months to shrink. These images show the minimum ice coverage during the summers of 1980, 2000 and 2020.

1980   **2000**   **2020**

By 2035, the Arctic Ocean is likely to be ice free in the summer.

Some Arctic species are struggling to survive. For example, as the snow in the Russian Arctic melts earlier, red knot chicks no longer hatch in time for the annual peak of insect food, which is triggered by the snowmelt.

But some see advantages in the ice melting. Melting ice will make it quicker and cheaper to transport goods through the Arctic Ocean.

Countries that stretch into the Arctic are competing for access to its resources and new shipping routes.

Melting land and sea ice is raising the sea level around the globe. Since 1880, the sea has risen up to 24cm (9in), and geographers predict that it could rise a further 1m (3ft) by 2100.

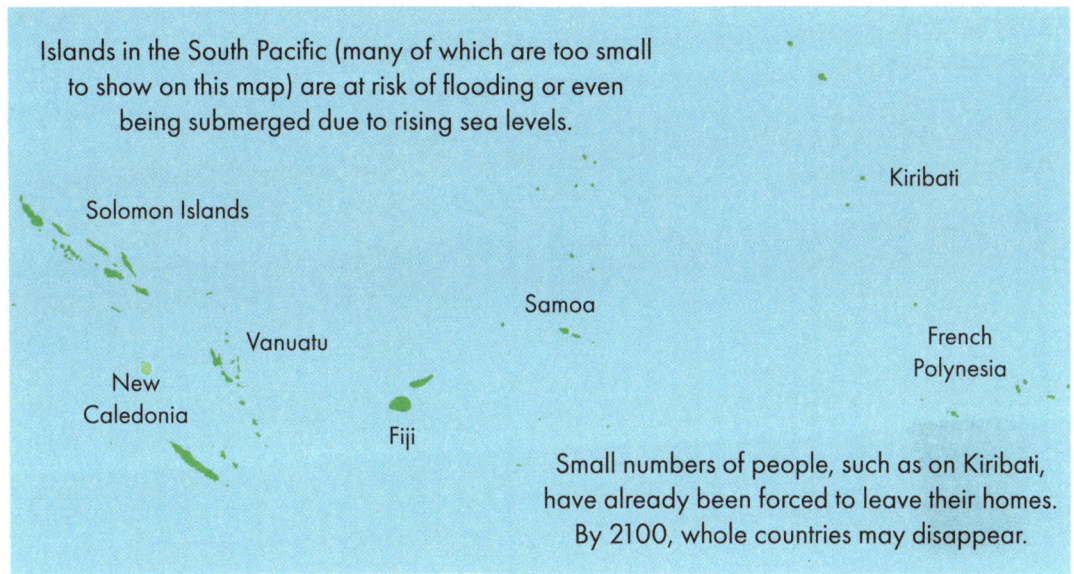

Islands in the South Pacific (many of which are too small to show on this map) are at risk of flooding or even being submerged due to rising sea levels.

Kiribati

Solomon Islands

Samoa

Vanuatu

French Polynesia

New Caledonia

Fiji

Small numbers of people, such as on Kiribati, have already been forced to leave their homes. By 2100, whole countries may disappear.

Every coastline will be affected by rising sea levels. Some areas will be worn away or **eroded** due to higher waters. Flooding will become more common, and many homes, roads and habitats will be destroyed.

If steps aren't taken to slow down global heating, scientists expect the sea levels around the city of New York to rise significantly.

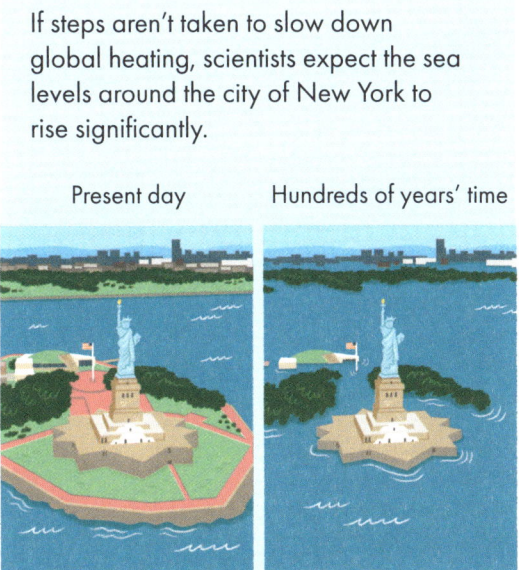

Present day | Hundreds of years' time

The city has invested billions in building a flood protection system in preparation.

By 2050, most of the city of Jakarta in Indonesia (a city of of around 11 million) will be under water, due to a combination of rising sea levels and the city sinking. Indonesia plans to move its capital to higher ground on another of its islands.

Running rivers

A river, such as the Ganges in Asia, is a lifeline to people and wildlife. Geographers are interested in how rivers flow and change – and how rivers affect people, and people affect rivers.

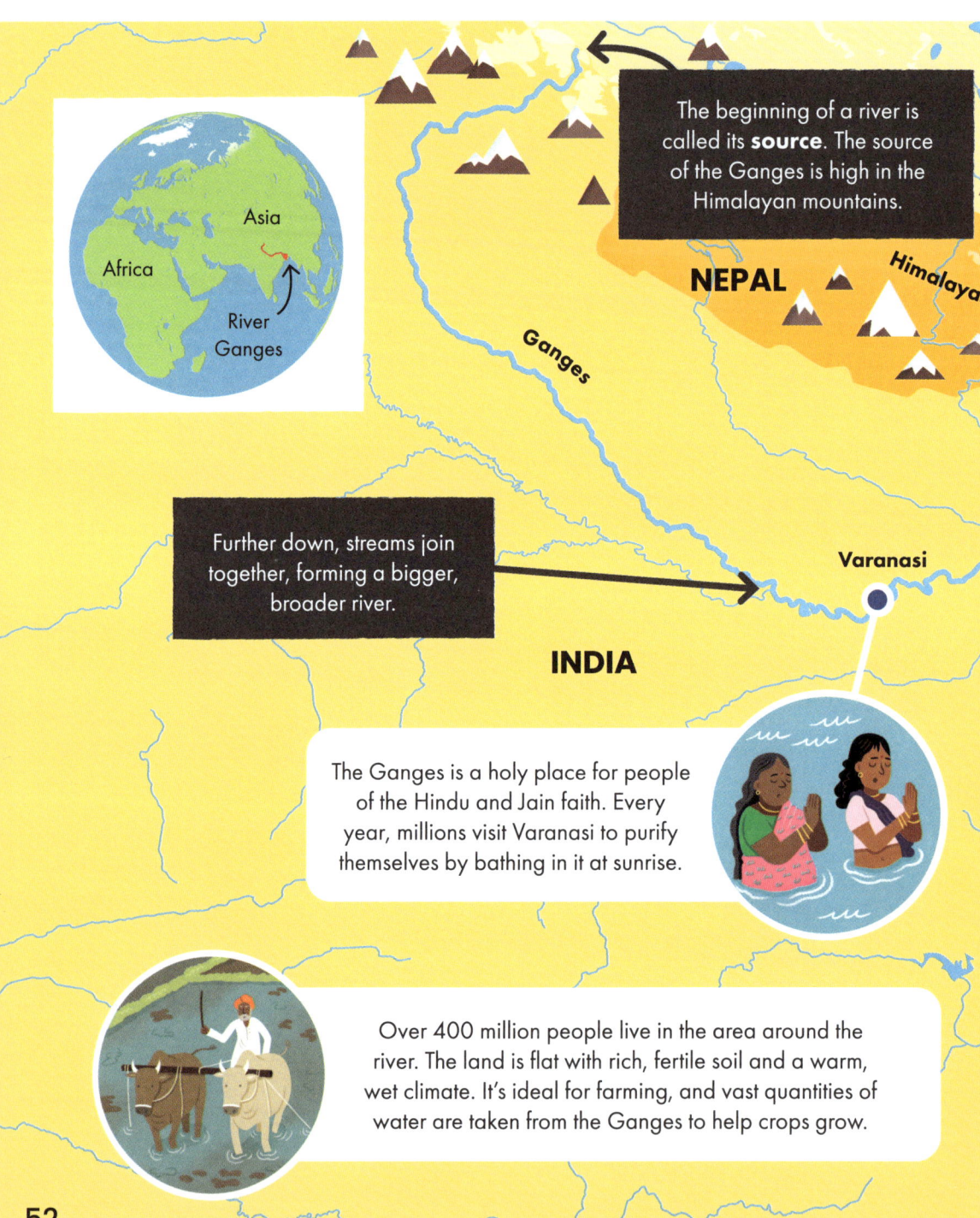

Human impact

Humans impact the river in so many different ways. Sewage, plastic and industrial waste make the Ganges one of the most polluted rivers in the world.

By the time the river flows into Bangladesh from India, the water is slow and very polluted, making it less useful. This leads to tensions between the two countries.

And global heating is causing the icy Himalayan glaciers that feed the Ganges to shrink. Scientists think this will result in decreased water levels over time.

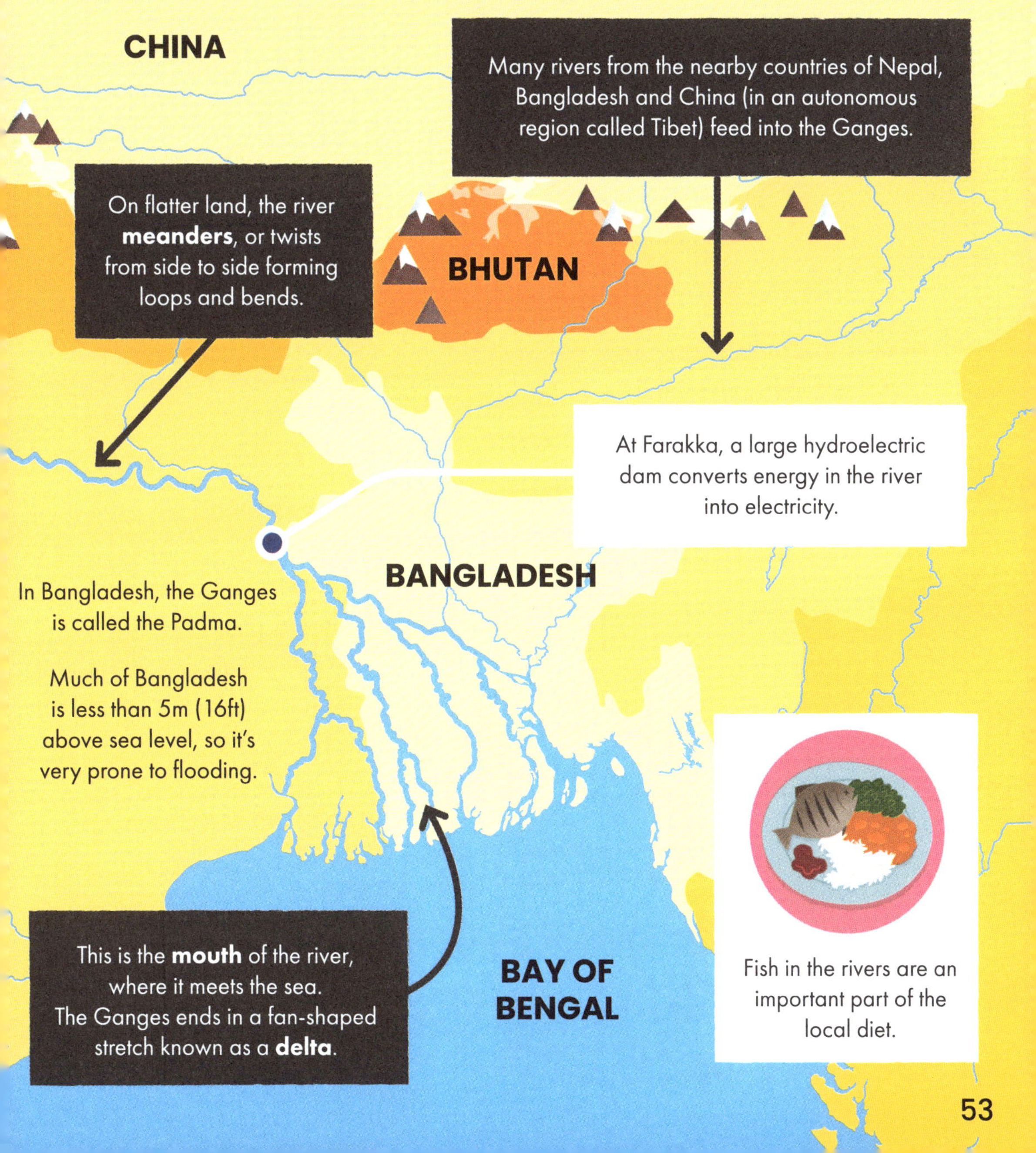

CHINA

Many rivers from the nearby countries of Nepal, Bangladesh and China (in an autonomous region called Tibet) feed into the Ganges.

On flatter land, the river **meanders**, or twists from side to side forming loops and bends.

BHUTAN

At Farakka, a large hydroelectric dam converts energy in the river into electricity.

BANGLADESH

In Bangladesh, the Ganges is called the Padma.

Much of Bangladesh is less than 5m (16ft) above sea level, so it's very prone to flooding.

This is the **mouth** of the river, where it meets the sea. The Ganges ends in a fan-shaped stretch known as a **delta**.

BAY OF BENGAL

Fish in the rivers are an important part of the local diet.

Water, water everywhere?

Fresh water is absolutely essential for human life. But across the world, access to water is unequal. This makes it a key issue for geographers to understand and manage.

The world population is growing – and so is the demand for water to drink, wash, make things and grow food.

Most freshwater use is for growing food – about two thirds of the total.

Already, more than half of humans live in places where the supply of water cannot meet demand – or won't be able to for much longer.

When more fresh water is drawn from the ground or a river to grow crops – or for any purpose – than is naturally replaced, it can cause all kinds of problems.

It can lead to the soil drying out and becoming dusty – a situation geographers call **drought**.

Droughts occur naturally, but in the past 40 years, the areas of Earth severely affected by drought have doubled to include more than 30% of the world's land.

A long period of drought can turn fertile land into a desert where little can grow. This can lead to food shortages and famines.

Taking too much water from the ground can cause the ground to sink...

...or it can cause seawater to seep into underground water stores, making them undrinkable.

Too salty!

Until recently, it was very hard for people to settle in areas without a reliable freshwater supply. But technology is changing this – just look at Qatar!

Qatar has no rivers and very little rain – barely any fresh water at all. In 1940, a population of just 10,000 lived in small settlements based near water sources.

Today, the country boasts huge cities and a population of almost three million. This is only possible because it has managed to develop a water supply.

Drinking water is made by removing salt from seawater in factories called **desalination plants**.

Waste water is cleaned and reused to water crops.

Some water is taken from underground water supplies called **aquifers**. But if overused, these will run out.

Wow, it sounds like desalination could solve all you humans' water problems.

If only it could... Desalination plants are *extremely* expensive to set up. They use LOTS of energy and make the remaining water supply much saltier. So although it's worked for Qatar so far, it's not a solution for everyone.

Doha seafront, Qatar

CHAPTER 4
Homes, towns, cities

Over the last hundred years, there has been a massive change in the way people live. Population growth has rocketed and cities have expanded. Many are still growing, especially in parts of Africa and Asia. But, in some of the world's richest countries, cities are shrinking, as people have smaller families or move out to the countryside.

To examine these changes, geographers distinguish between **urban** areas – where people live closely in towns and cities – and **rural** areas – in the countryside. However, the definitions are not fixed, and what is urban in one country might be considered rural in another.

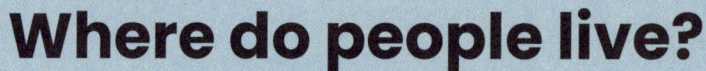

As the world changes and industries boom, fail or move abroad, some settlements expand and others decline. Geographers are interested in how settlements change, particularly cities – turn the page to find out more...

What is a city?

When does a town become a city? Sometimes, it's all about how many people live there. But a small place might be a city, if the government is there. All cities are different, but many share similar characteristics.

How do places grow?

Towns and cities expand in different ways, due to road and rail routes, jobs and the changing tastes of the people who live there. Geographers look for patterns in the way that settlements grow.

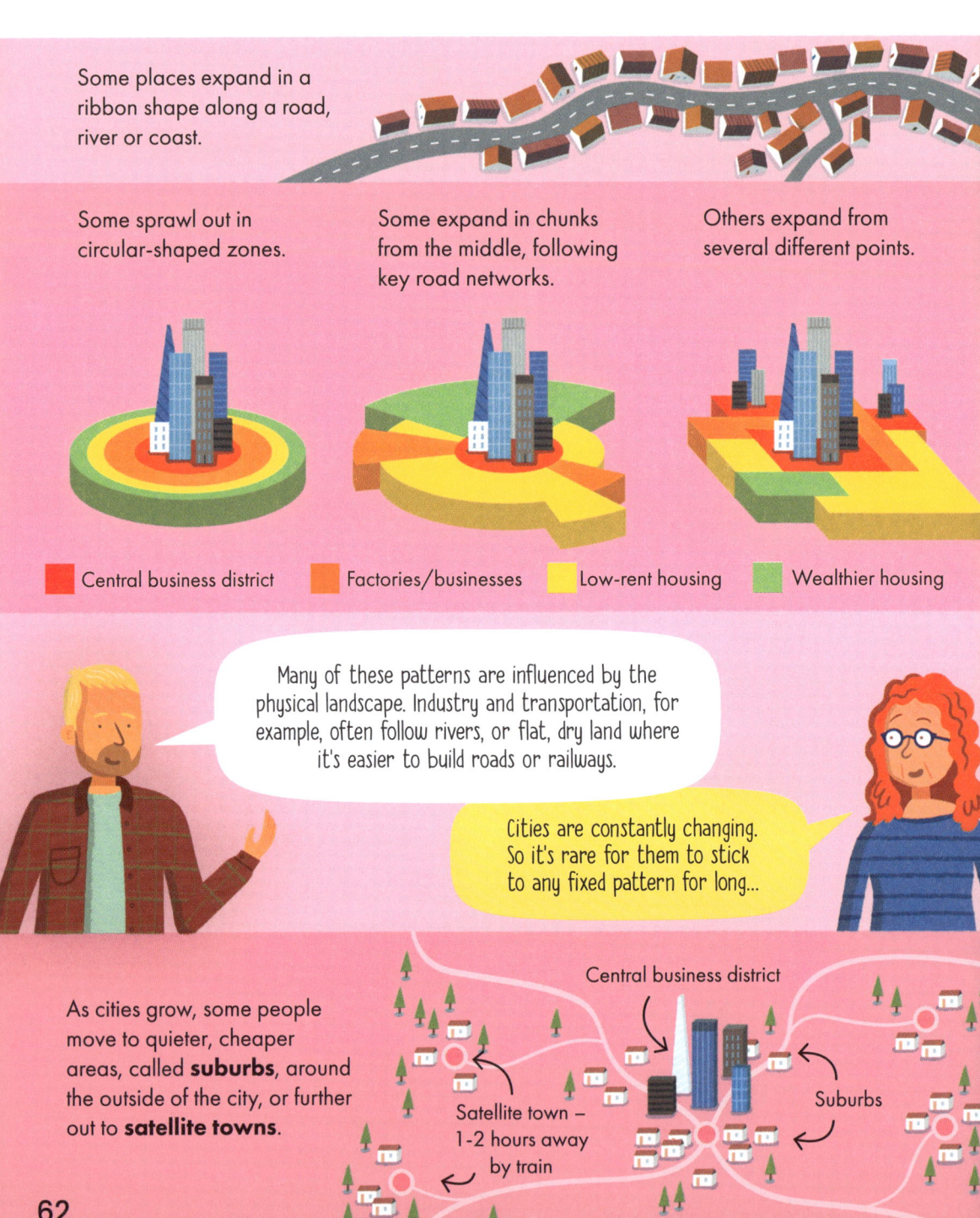

Some places expand in a ribbon shape along a road, river or coast.

Some sprawl out in circular-shaped zones.

Some expand in chunks from the middle, following key road networks.

Others expand from several different points.

- Central business district
- Factories/businesses
- Low-rent housing
- Wealthier housing

Many of these patterns are influenced by the physical landscape. Industry and transportation, for example, often follow rivers, or flat, dry land where it's easier to build roads or railways.

Cities are constantly changing. So it's rare for them to stick to any fixed pattern for long...

As cities grow, some people move to quieter, cheaper areas, called **suburbs**, around the outside of the city, or further out to **satellite towns**.

Central business district

Satellite town – 1-2 hours away by train

Suburbs

Different kinds of cities

Some cities grow in bursts as a result of a thriving industry or trade. Others are planned in specific shapes, with roads and areas for parks and shops.

In 1957, Lúcio Costa and Oscar Niemeyer designed a new capital for Brazil in the shape of a plane.

Plan for Brasília, 1957

It's like a plane or a cross, the meeting of two main roads, with lots of space.

Satellite view of Brasília today

Brasília is now Brazil's third biggest city after São Paulo and Rio de Janeiro. It has grown hugely beyond its original plan, as people flocked to the city and began setting up their own places to live. Geographers describe these sort of city add-ons as **informal settlements**.

Population: 4.9 million

Timbuktu, Mali, on the edge of the Sahara desert, grew rich as a place for trading salt, gold and books. It has three historic mosques and is a hub for Islamic learning. Recently, fighting in the region has caused thousands to flee the city.

Population: 32,000

Historic Timbuktu

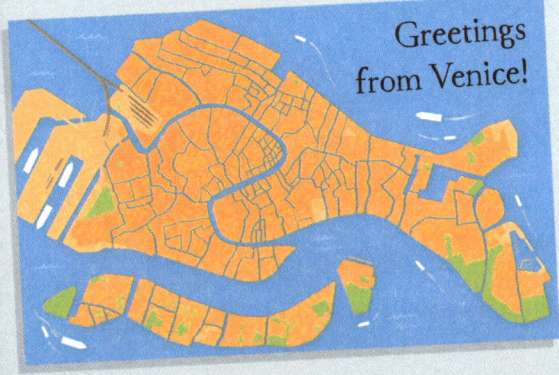

Greetings from Venice!

Venice, Italy, was built on 118 small islands, separated by canals and linked by 400 bridges. Today, it thrives on tourism, but it's under threat from rising sea levels.

Population: 641,000

Where do cities start and end?

Long ago, many cities were built within an outer wall that created a clear boundary. Today, as cities sprawl further and further out into green spaces, or decline and shrink, it's far from clear where any boundary lies.

"The houses are very spaced out here, and there's a lake and a retail park. Is this still in the city?"

"I think it's not... yet. They're about to build a new train station and 1,000 homes that will join this area to a more built-up one, and perhaps then it will count as being in the city."

Without a clear boundary, however, it's impossible to determine a city's population or area, the number of schools and what services it needs. So people who run cities have to decide on boundaries somewhere.

"What is the population of Tokyo, capital city of Japan?"

"If we draw around the more densely populated areas, the population is nine million."

"But if we include the less densely populated areas, the population is 37 million."

Changing fortunes

When industries boom, they attract thousands of workers to a city. But if they fail, or move to other places, workers can be left jobless, shops close down, buildings decay, and poverty and social problems increase.

The coal, steel and car industries are booming and people are flocking to live in this city.

Industries have shut down, buildings are empty and thousands of people are out of work.

However, just as quickly as areas decay, they can also be regenerated, often with the help of big projects and inventive ideas by town planners, architects and landscape designers.

I'm a town planner. I look at ways to improve city spaces for people. I select new developments that work well with the local area. We also restore old buildings of historical or cultural interest.

Downtown Seoul, South Korea, lost much of its population in the 1980s and '90s, and many of its buildings became derelict. The Cheonggyecheon project, begun in 2003, saw the transformation of a 10-lane roadway into a vast green public space with a river, attracting thousands of visitors and new investment.

From rural to urban life

Around 250 years ago, the vast majority of people in the world lived in rural communities. But over the next few decades, a series of changes encouraged more and more people to move into towns and cities...

Timeline of urban growth

1750

Only 3% of the world's population live in cities. Most people farm the land and make clothes and goods by hand.

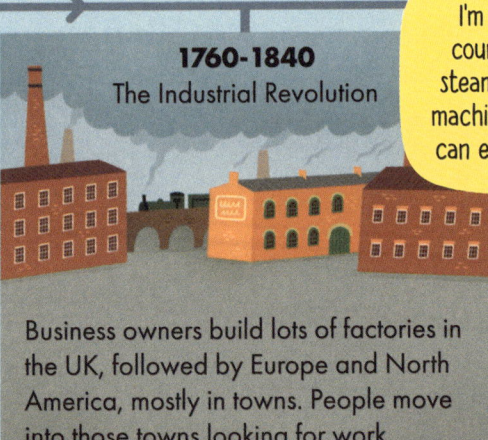

1760-1840
The Industrial Revolution

Business owners build lots of factories in the UK, followed by Europe and North America, mostly in towns. People move into those towns looking for work.

I'm moving from the country to work on a steam-powered weaving machine in a factory, so I can earn a regular wage.

Making sense of change

Geographers try to find out what makes cities grow or shrink.

What makes cities grow?

- Jobs
- **Good health** — Better food and health mean people live longer.
- High birth rate
- Affordable homes
- **Amenities** — Schools, parks, cafés
- High wages
- Good transportation
- **Education** — Knowledge and skills boost business and the economy.
- Stable government
- New opportunities

1900

Healthcare and hygiene improve. More children survive and adults live longer. The population booms in London, New York, Paris, Berlin and Tokyo.

1950

A third of the world lives in cities. New York and Tokyo become **megacities** – cities with over 10 million people.

1990

The number of megacities rises to 10:

- Tokyo
- Osaka
- New York
- Mexico City
- São Paulo
- Mumbai
- Buenos Aires
- Calcutta
- Los Angeles
- Seoul

2020

Over half the world's population lives in cities. The fastest urban growth shifts to Asia and Africa.

In 2023, there are 33 megacities, but some cities are shrinking.

By 2050, two thirds of all people are expected to live in cities.

What makes cities shrink?

A city can gain a good or bad reputation, which also affects whether people WANT to live there.

- **Low birth rate**
- **Pollution** — Dirty air or water, too much noise
- **Over-crowding**
- **High prices**
- **No jobs**
- **Desire for more living space**
- **Few opportunities**
- **War**
- **Crime**
- **Natural disasters** — Earthquakes, floods volcanoes, hurricanes

Bigger and bigger

Geographers use population data to look at trends and make projections about how places might change in the future as their populations grow.

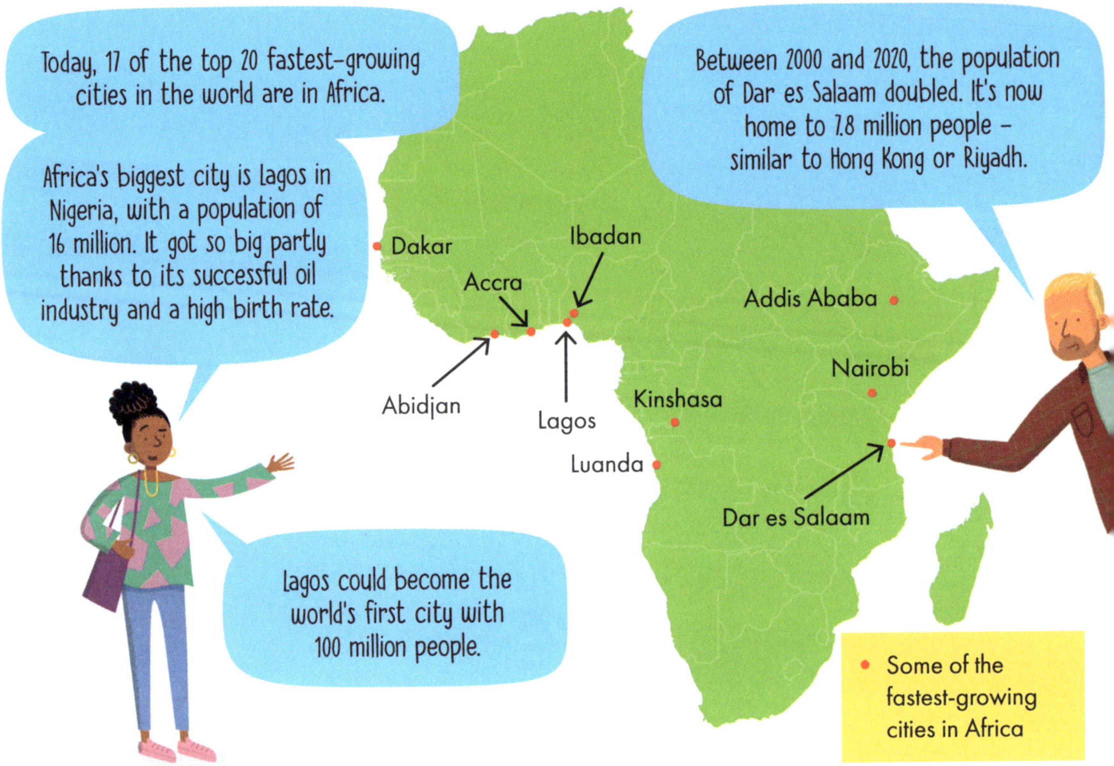

Today, 17 of the top 20 fastest-growing cities in the world are in Africa.

Africa's biggest city is Lagos in Nigeria, with a population of 16 million. It got so big partly thanks to its successful oil industry and a high birth rate.

Between 2000 and 2020, the population of Dar es Salaam doubled. It's now home to 7.8 million people – similar to Hong Kong or Riyadh.

Dakar • Ibadan • Accra • Abidjan • Lagos • Kinshasa • Luanda • Addis Ababa • Nairobi • Dar es Salaam

Lagos could become the world's first city with 100 million people.

• Some of the fastest-growing cities in Africa

New towns and cities

Some countries have created towns and cities from scratch by selecting areas to develop, building roads and houses and creating opportunities for growth.

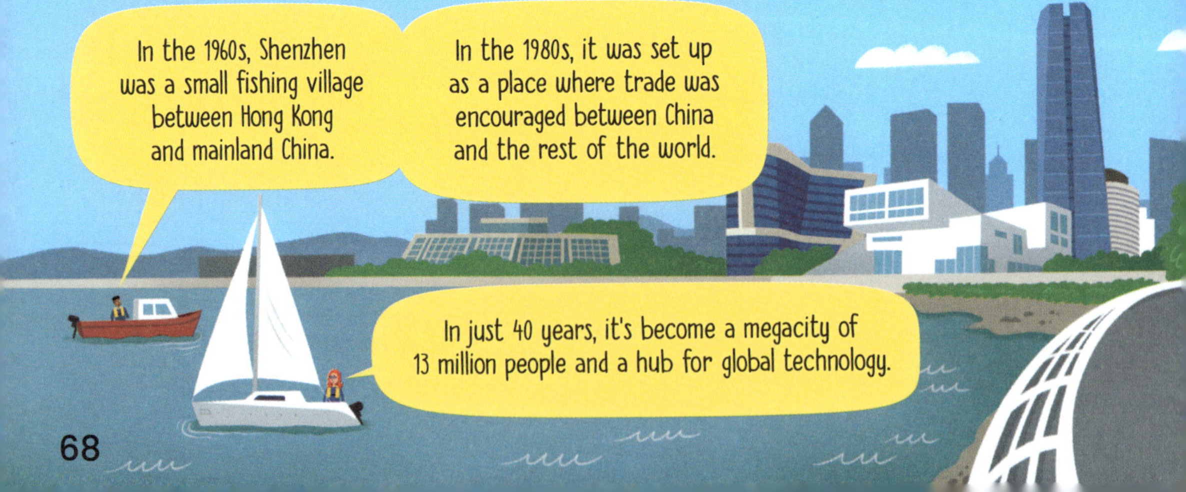

In the 1960s, Shenzhen was a small fishing village between Hong Kong and mainland China.

In the 1980s, it was set up as a place where trade was encouraged between China and the rest of the world.

In just 40 years, it's become a megacity of 13 million people and a hub for global technology.

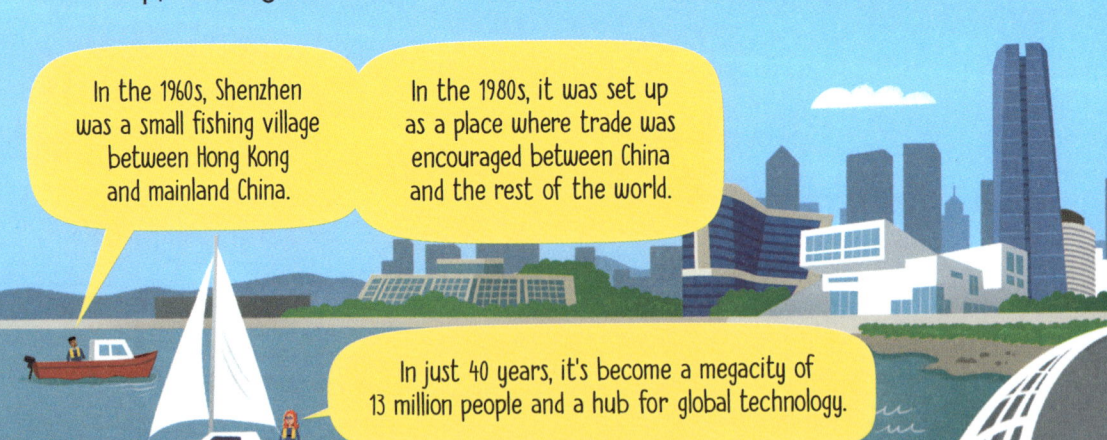

Higher and higher

Here's another thing that has helped cities grow: using new technology to make taller and taller buildings.

The technology to construct high buildings with steel and concrete led to the first skyscrapers in the US over 100 years ago.

Building high-rise apartments created much denser urban areas throughout the world.

New styles of building also led to a massive change in the appearance of inner-city areas.

The power of art and culture

Urban areas develop and change in multiple ways. Some have been transformed by art, architecture and even food.

In the 1980s, Bilbao in Spain was a run-down industrial city that had once thrived on steel and ship-building.

The building of the Guggenheim Museum in 1997 and the opening up of the waterfront area transformed the city.

Since its completion, the art gallery has attracted over a million visitors a year and given a huge boost to the city's economy.

People also flock to Bilbao for the quality of its local food. Several of the world's top-rated restaurants are located in the area.

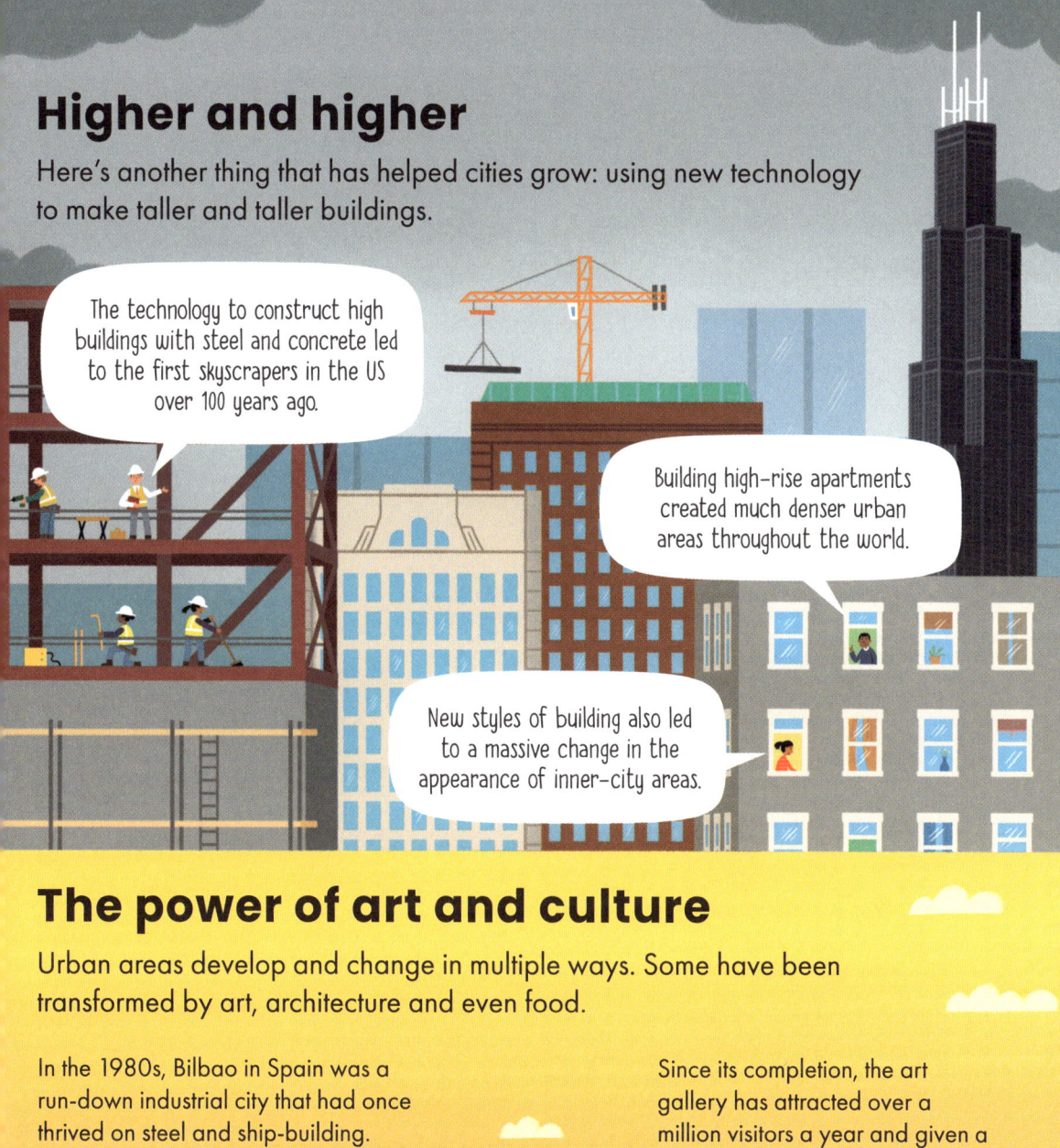

Moving around in cities

To run smoothly, cities need a highly organized transportation system that allows huge numbers of people and goods to move about at all hours of the day. But transportation can also cause problems that need to be solved.

Imagine you're a member of a local council, meeting to discuss ways to improve roads in your area.

I propose a super-fast highway, so people can drive quickly in and out of the city. We must keep traffic flowing!

But that will cut through local communities and encourage more cars, traffic and pollution.

Instead of new roads, I think we need a better bus network, and new, faster underground trains, to deter people from driving!

I think our priority should be to stop using any vehicles – car, buses or trains – that burn fuel and warm the planet.

Digging tunnels is hugely expensive and time-consuming. Do we have enough money to consider updating the metro system?

What do you think?

It's often geographers who come up with solutions. They look at proposals and weigh up the pros and cons. They also study how the politics of the local government affects urban planning. Some local governments focus more on projects to boost business, while others spend more on improving quality of life.

Green and blue spaces

Central city areas change rapidly, often within a few years. Green and blue spaces, such as parks and lakes, are good for people's health. So town planners constantly look at ways to increase their use in urban areas.

Improving links

Some urban geographers look at the details of how cities work, while others focus on the bigger picture. This includes finding ways to improve links between cities or countries, and helping poorer areas prosper.

The Øresund road and railway bridge between the Danish capital, Copenhagen, and Malmö in Sweden was built in 2000. It has cut travel time, boosted trade and improved relations between the countries.

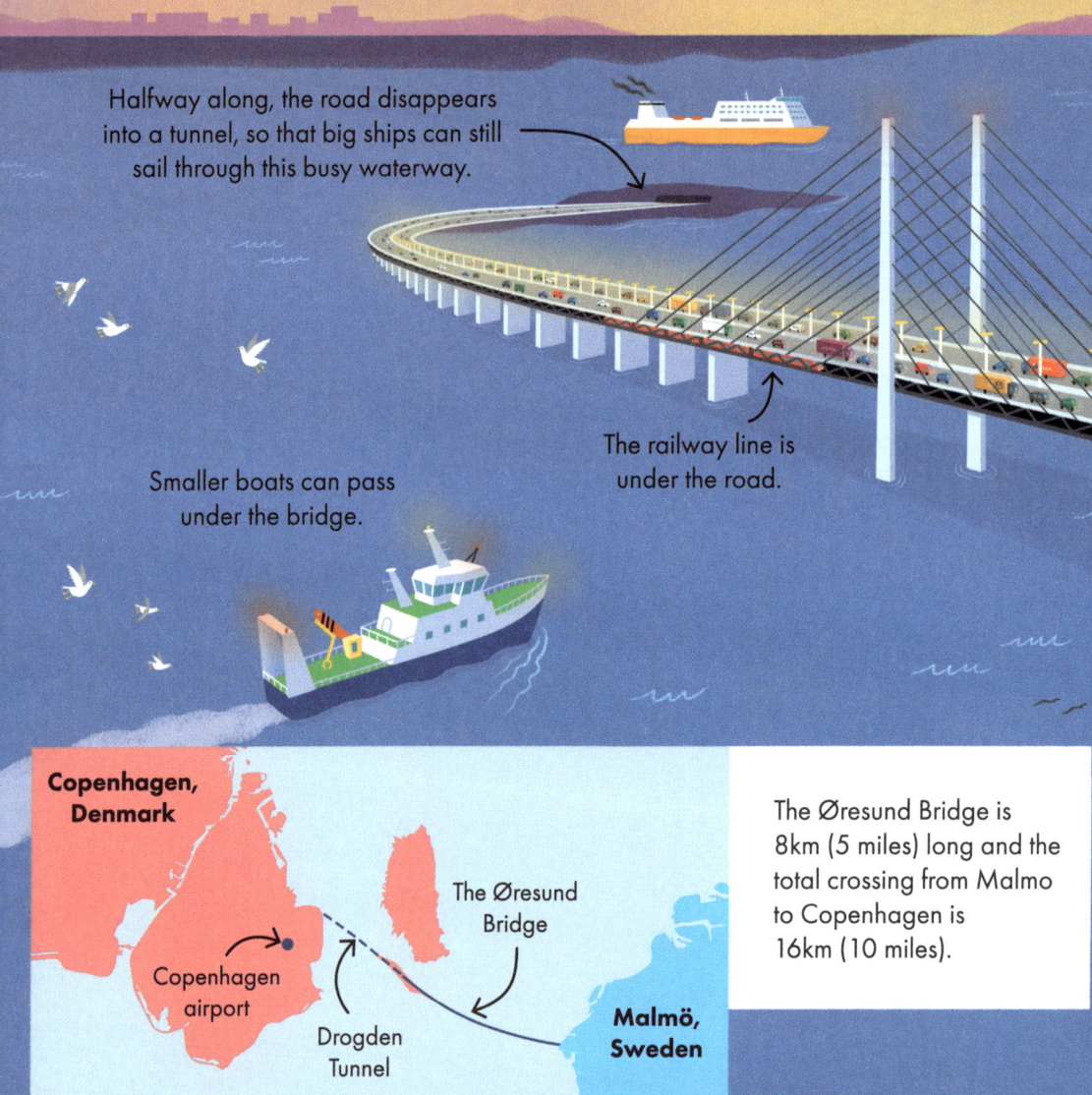

Halfway along, the road disappears into a tunnel, so that big ships can still sail through this busy waterway.

The railway line is under the road.

Smaller boats can pass under the bridge.

Copenhagen, Denmark

Copenhagen airport

Drogden Tunnel

The Øresund Bridge

Malmö, Sweden

The Øresund Bridge is 8km (5 miles) long and the total crossing from Malmo to Copenhagen is 16km (10 miles).

Rural areas

Around the world, over three billion people live in rural areas. There's a lot to learn about how they live there, especially about how the landscape and their lifestyles are changing.

"This agricultural landscape with walks and woodland is beautiful. Why can't it stay like this forever?"

"There's a lot of poverty in the area and few jobs. Farmers used to employ hundreds of people, but now the work is done mostly by machine. An online shopping company wants to build a huge warehouse here that will create hundreds of jobs."

"But once you build in this landscape, you change it forever. Millions of people visit the area for its beauty. We should preserve it for future generations."

"But we need to create new houses and energy as well as work. We want young people to be able to afford to live here, too."

"OK, that is a dilemma. But what about food? Building on this land means people can't use the soil to grow things. And THAT means we'll have to import food, which costs more money, and increases pollution..."

"You're right, that's something people should think about carefully, too!"

To protect the best farmland, governments do surveys to examine the quality of their soil. Development might be banned in regions with the most productive soil. But there may be mounting pressure to build in less fertile areas, especially where the population is expanding.

Moving out of the city

In the past, many people moved into cities to find work. But nowadays the internet allows many people to work from home. Geographers are watching as this massive technological change is affecting how and where people live.

"I can be in meetings all day without leaving my house. When the internet is working, that is."

Campaign for fast broadband

"I can buy and sell things, and arrange to have them shipped all over the world, without going near a city."

"My company shut down its central office during the Covid-19 pandemic. Now we all work from home."

Geographers are interested in what it's like for people living in an area and why they move or live there. To find out, they conduct questionnaires and look at data such as changes in house prices.

What residents say about life in Puddleton village

"It's peaceful and beautiful. We're lucky to be able to choose where to live and we chose HERE."

"I moved here to work as a kayak instructor – but I only get enough work when people come to stay in the summertime."

"I want to move out from my parents, but can't afford my own place. There aren't many buses and the internet is too slow. I feel stuck."

"My family has had a sheep farm here for years. I love it, but the price of animal feed is rising and it's hard to find young workers. Luckily I get some money from the government or I'd have to close down."

House prices in Puddleton

(Cost vs Year — rising trend)

"Why is it too expensive for some people to buy a house in this village?"

"Wealthy people have been moving here, which has pushed house prices up."

CHAPTER 5
How money and power shape the world

It's not just mountain ranges and rivers that carve up the landscape. Politics does too. "Politics" means the things that the people in charge decide to do.

Politics most clearly divides up the world through boundaries called **borders** that separate countries. Borders have HUGE consequences. They determine which countries have access to water, oil and other resources, and they dictate where people can live, work and travel to.

Governments' actions shape the world too – but some countries' governments do so far more than others. A few countries, known as **superpowers**, are so large and powerful that their actions influence many other countries.

Countries and borders

The world is divided up into around 200 countries, also called nations or states. But people disagree about borders and what is or isn't a country. Maps showing countries and borders are known as **political maps**.

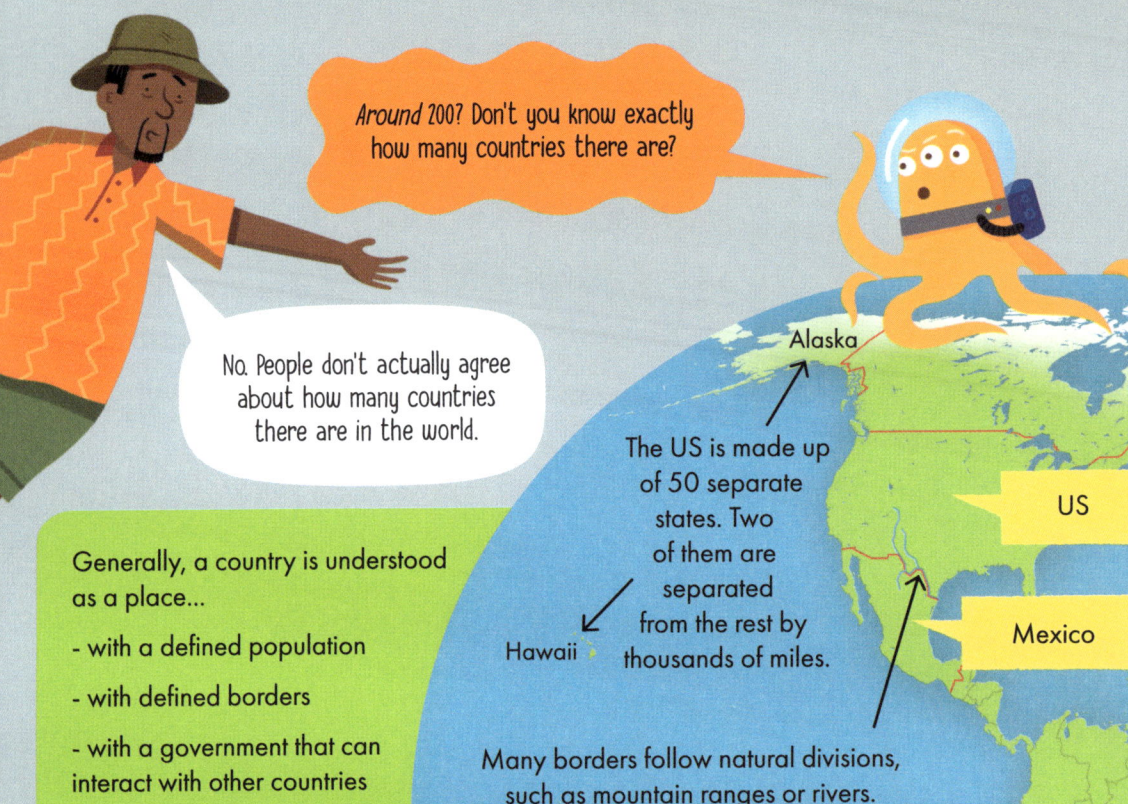

Around 200? Don't you know exactly how many countries there are?

No. People don't actually agree about how many countries there are in the world.

Generally, a country is understood as a place...
- with a defined population
- with defined borders
- with a government that can interact with other countries
- that is recognized as a country by other countries.

So some places are only partially recognized countries – for instance, only 98 states consider Kosovo a country.

Some people think a country exists whether or not it is recognized by other states, as long as most people who live in that place think it's a separate country.

The US is made up of 50 separate states. Two of them are separated from the rest by thousands of miles.

Many borders follow natural divisions, such as mountain ranges or rivers. For instance, part of the border between the US and Mexico follows the Rio Grande river.

But the Rio Grande has changed course numerous times, which has led to disputes between the US and Mexico.

BOLIVIA once had 400km (250 miles) of coast, but lost it to Chile during the War of the Pacific (1879–1884).

Borders might look straightforward on a map, but up close, and especially to the people who live near them, they rarely are. There are more than 100 ongoing border disputes.

Even agreed-upon borders can be complicated. The official border between Belgium and the Netherlands runs through the town of Baarle and divides living rooms and cafés.

Baarle

I'm in Belgium, but my husband's in the Netherlands.

KOSOVO declared independence from Serbia in 2008, but Serbia doesn't recognize its independence.

RUSSIA is the largest country in the world by area.

INDIA probably has the largest population in the world – it's hard to be certain.

Island countries, such as **MADAGASCAR**, have borders with other countries, but they are at sea, not on land.

There aren't any countries in Antarctica. It is governed by around 30 countries, according to an agreement known as the Antarctic Treaty System.

ANTARCTICA

Different countries draw political maps differently, depending on which countries they recognize. Also, political maps don't stay the same for long, because borders shift by agreement or through conflict.

Trading

To get everything it needs, almost every nation has to buy goods from other countries. To pay for this, they sell goods they DO have. This exchange is called **trade** and it dates back to the earliest civilizations. Here's how it works.

Some countries have become better at producing certain goods than others. They exchange these goods for those that other countries are better at producing.

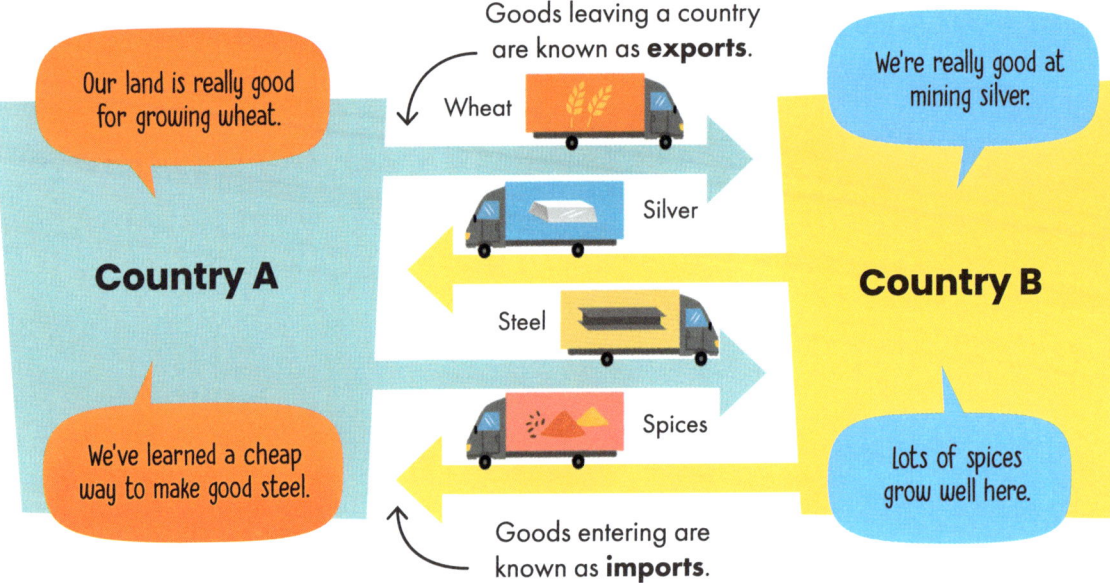

Trade can bring countries together, as they come to rely on each other for things they need – or it can push them apart...

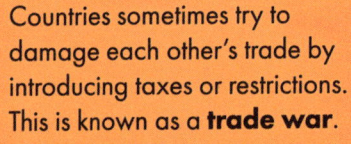

Countries sometimes try to damage each other's trade by introducing taxes or restrictions. This is known as a **trade war**.

"Country B makes silver so much more cheaply than we do. All *our* silver companies are going out of business!

I'm increasing taxes on silver imports, so *their* silver becomes more expensive and people buy OUR silver again."

"Well then *I'm* going to raise taxes on wheat imports from Country A."

How and what a country trades has a huge impact. Trade can make a country wealthy, or cause lots of problems. Trading relationships can even make a country more influential in world affairs.

For instance, some countries rely heavily on exporting a particular product. If demand for that product – or its price – falls, that country's income drops suddenly too.

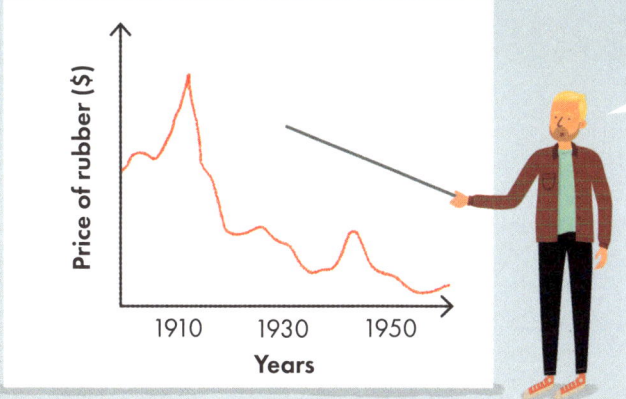

In 1900, Brazil was the world's main supplier of natural rubber.

But, within forty years, the market for Brazilian rubber collapsed. Southeast Asian rubber plantations began to produce rubber more cheaply, and then synthetic rubber was invented.

Being the main producer of certain goods in an area can put a country in a powerful position...

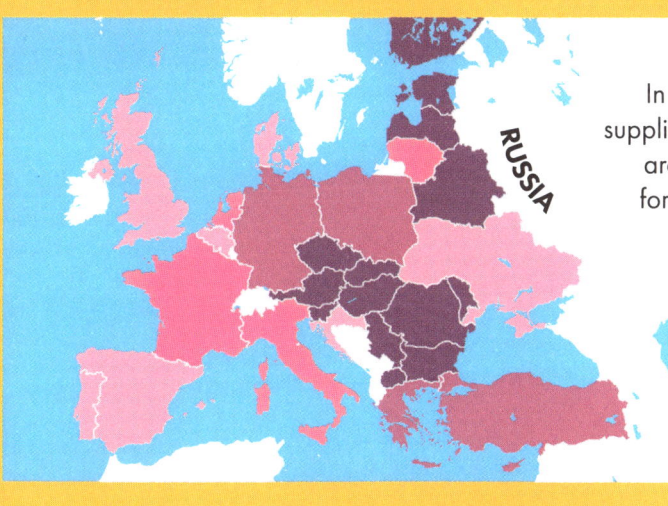

In 2021, Russia was the main supplier of gas to Europe. It supplied around 45% of Europe's gas, for around **US$55.5 billion**.

Some countries (shown in dark purple on this map) were completely dependent on Russian gas.

In 2022, when Russia attacked Ukraine, some nearby countries were reluctant to show their disapproval. They feared that Russia might reduce their supply of gas or even cut it off entirely.

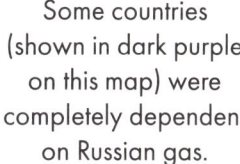

Understanding trade relationships is one way that **political geographers** make sense of the relationships between different regions and how they use their resources.

Strengths and weaknesses

Countries each have their own strengths and weaknesses at the same time. Here's how a geographer might study two very different countries.

SWITZERLAND

Switzerland is a relatively small, land-locked country, with lots of mountains and lakes.

Total area: 41,285km² (15,940 miles²)

The land isn't suited to growing food, and there are few **resources** buried in the ground.

There is, however, a lot of rain. This is collected in artificial lakes and used to generate pollution-free, green hydroelectric **energy**. Almost 60% of Switzerland's electricity is made this way.

Switzerland's **economy** is very strong. For the size of its population (8.7 million), it produces more expensive goods and products than almost anywhere else in the world.

NIGERIA

Nigeria is a large coastal country with one of the biggest river systems in the world.

Total area: 923,768km² (356,669 miles²)

There are rich supplies of **resources** – oil, natural gas, coal, tin, copper and iron – as well as lots of potential for generating renewable energy.

But having these resources isn't the whole story. Despite large supplies of fossil fuels, the way the **energy** supply is set up means people across the country often experience power cuts or other difficulties.

Nigeria's **economy** is the largest in Africa and growing. But it faces challenges...

One way to see how a country is doing financially is to look at its **economy**. A country's economy means how much money it makes from business and industry.

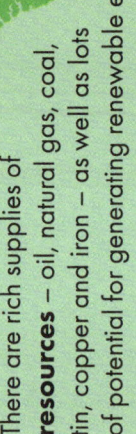

A deadly **disease** called malaria spreads all year round in the tropical climate. Medical treatment, time off work and lost tourism due to the disease costs Nigeria as much as US$700 million a year.

Unemployment is higher in Nigeria than Switzerland, and many skilled workers choose to leave the country to find work.

Nigeria's **population** is the seventh largest in the world, and growing fast. This means it has a young, energetic workforce, but there is also pressure on food and energy supplies, as well as schools, hospitals and other services.

Nigeria has been independent since 1960. Before that, the British government controlled it for around a hundred years.

The British exploited Nigeria's raw materials and people for Britain's benefit, rather than focusing on the needs of Nigeria's people.

A country's **history** can be a strength or create challenges. Long-term independence and secure, stable governments allow countries to develop in a way that serves their interests.

Lots of people in Switzerland are well educated and well trained in various jobs. Geographers say it has a *highly-skilled workforce*.

It produces sophisticated watches, medicines and other expensive products. Workers are paid well and there is very little unemployment.

However, the **population** in Switzerland is ageing and declining. That means the government has to find more and more money to support people financially after they retire, and to pay for healthcare as they age.

Switzerland has been independent since 1648. This has given the country hundreds of years to build up industries and businesses to serve its population's needs.

Globalization

In the last 50 years, economies, political systems and cultures around the world have become more and more interlinked – a process called **globalization**. Geographers are interested in the impact this has on places and how people and goods move around the world.

Globalization has changed how we live...

But globalization itself is nothing new. It's been going on for as long as people have made long journeys, taking their goods, ideas and culture with them.

Around 2,000 years ago, merchants began to trade along a network of routes. It became known as the *Silk Road* and connected parts of Europe, Africa and East Asia.

People got used to buying international products, from Chinese silk to European glass.

These routes also helped spread architectural styles, religious ideas, and even new methods of warfare, such as gunpowder.

However, over the past 50 years or so, globalization has been happening faster than ever before, transforming how countries interact with each other and changing the way people live and work.

Trade

The amount of trade between different countries has more than *quadrupled* in the past 40 years. When countries trade with each other, they become financially interlinked, but also tend to forge stronger links in other areas, too, such as culture and politics.

Getting around

In 1700, it took two years to travel around the world by boat. Nowadays, it takes less than two days by plane.

Faster vehicles make it easier for people to travel and trade. For instance, farmers in Spain can sell their strawberries around the world, even though they're only good to eat for a few days.

Technology

The internet has made international business much easier. Money can be sent around the world with a few clicks, and people can log in to a meeting from wherever they are via video link.

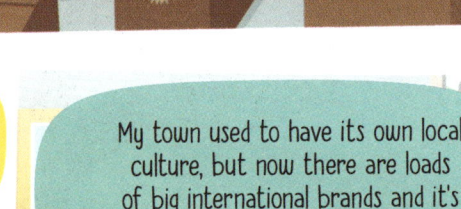

Superpowers

Some countries have far more influence in world affairs than others. They are good at protecting their interests and making the world work for them. The most powerful are known as **superpowers**.

The most influential countries usually have strengths in lots of different areas. Take the US, thought by many to be the biggest superpower.

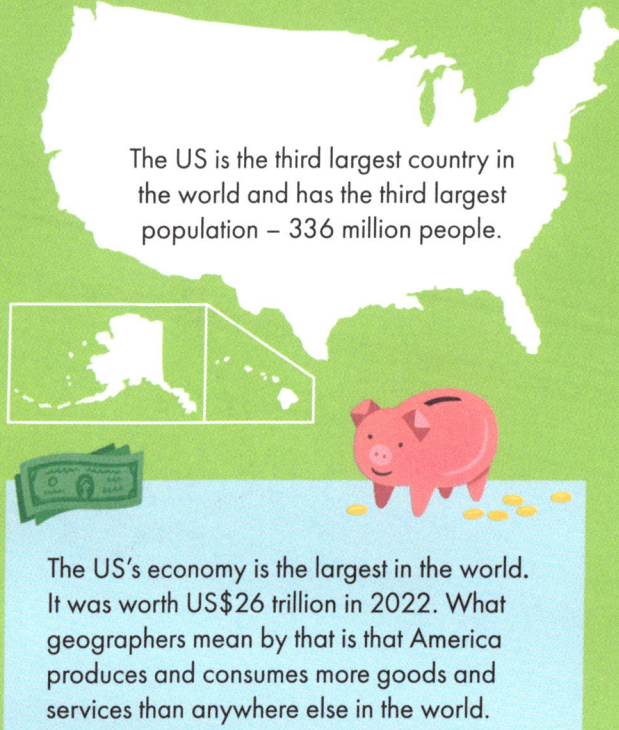

The US is the third largest country in the world and has the third largest population – 336 million people.

The US's economy is the largest in the world. It was worth US$26 trillion in 2022. What geographers mean by that is that America produces and consumes more goods and services than anywhere else in the world.

The US has the strongest armed forces in the world. It is one of just nine countries with deadly nuclear weapons. It has around 600 military bases all over the world.

This allows it to protect its interests all over the globe. It also deters other countries from acting in a way that could go against the wishes of the US.

How does the US influence other countries?

The US can carry out, or threaten, military action, or change how it trades to damage a country's economy.

Also, this influence can be more subtle. The popularity of US movies, brands, lifestyle and culture around the world can bring other countries closer to the US way of doing things and seeing the world.

It's hard for small countries with small economies to make their voices heard on the world stage. One way for them to get around this is by forming partnerships with other countries and signing agreements.

When lots of countries come together and act as one, it greatly increases their power. The **European Union (EU)** is considered by many to be a superpower. Compared to any single country, this alliance of 27 countries has...

 ...more bargaining power. It can make better trade deals with other countries.

 ...more influence. Although it doesn't have its own army, other countries pay attention to its position on key issues such as war and climate change.

 ...a bigger economy. The EU is the third largest economy in the world.

 ...slower decision-making. All its members have to be in complete agreement before it takes certain actions. This can make the EU appear weak and divided.

Countries aren't the only players in world affairs; international organizations also influence world events. One of the most important is the **United Nations (UN)**. It was set up in 1945, after the devastation of the Second World War, with the goal of promoting world peace. Almost every country is a member.

When countries disagree or conflict breaks out, the UN encourages the groups involved to negotiate with each other.

The UN can also deploy troops and police to keep the peace. The troops come from member states and don't take sides. They can only use force to defend themselves.

The UN sounds a bit like a referee for world affairs.

But its hands are sometimes tied, as powerful countries can vote to block action they don't agree with.

People moving around

People are on the move as never before. Some move for work or study, some to be near family, and some to escape violence, floods or famine. The movement of people from one place to another is known as **migration**.

Is migration a new thing that humans do?

No! People have been migrating throughout human history – that's around 300,000 years.

Are people migrating within a country or to new countries?

Both. In 2020, 281 million people migrated to a new country – 3.6% of the global population. That's up from 2.5% in 2000.

Where are they going from, and where do they go to?

That's the question lots of geographers study! But finding exact answers is not always easy, because some people are not recorded on any official lists...

In 2020, more people migrated from India than any other country. Many of these migrants went to countries where governments encourage workers to fill job vacancies, such as the United Arab Emirates or Saudi Arabia. People who move to a new country by choice are known as **immigrants**.

United States

In 2020, the US was the most popular destination for immigrants.

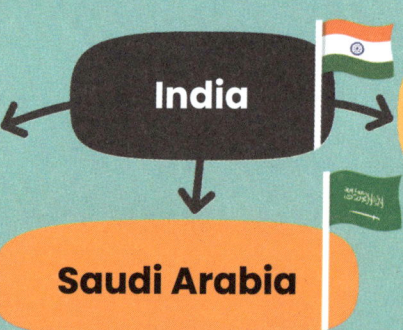

India

Saudi Arabia

Around 2.5 million Indians live in Saudi Arabia.

United Arab Emirates

In the UAE, over 88% of the population are immigrants, mostly from India.

Migration routes are constantly shifting in response to a changing world. Sometimes, new routes open up for large numbers all at once. These are for people escaping from harm, rather than by choice. People who move countries for safety are called **refugees**. Here are a few reasons why this happens.

War
Home town is under attack.

Persecution
At risk of being arrested or even killed because of lifestyle or personal beliefs

Natural disasters
Home town destroyed by earthquake

Geographers try to find out hard facts about what impact immigration has on places and people.

"Some of the biggest companies in the world, such as Apple, Google and Amazon, were started by immigrants or the children of immigrants."

"I'm looking at the effect of immigrants on schools, health and housing."

"I'm making a list of new cultural events, restaurants and small businesses started by immigrants in the area."

"I'm asking other immigrants about their experiences. I want to find out what services are available, such as language tuition."

CHAPTER 6
Improving lives

Development can be described as any improvement in a country's living standards or quality of life. It includes progress in all sorts of areas, from education and health, to job opportunities and personal freedoms.

What does that have to do with geography? Well, it's part of geography to examine and measure the differences in development within countries and around the world. Using this data, it's possible to assess which places have a better quality of life than others, and find out why.

Measuring development

To show the progress of a country's development, geographers use measures, known as **indicators**, and compare them over time. There are hundreds of different indicators, each with their own pros and cons. Here are just a few.

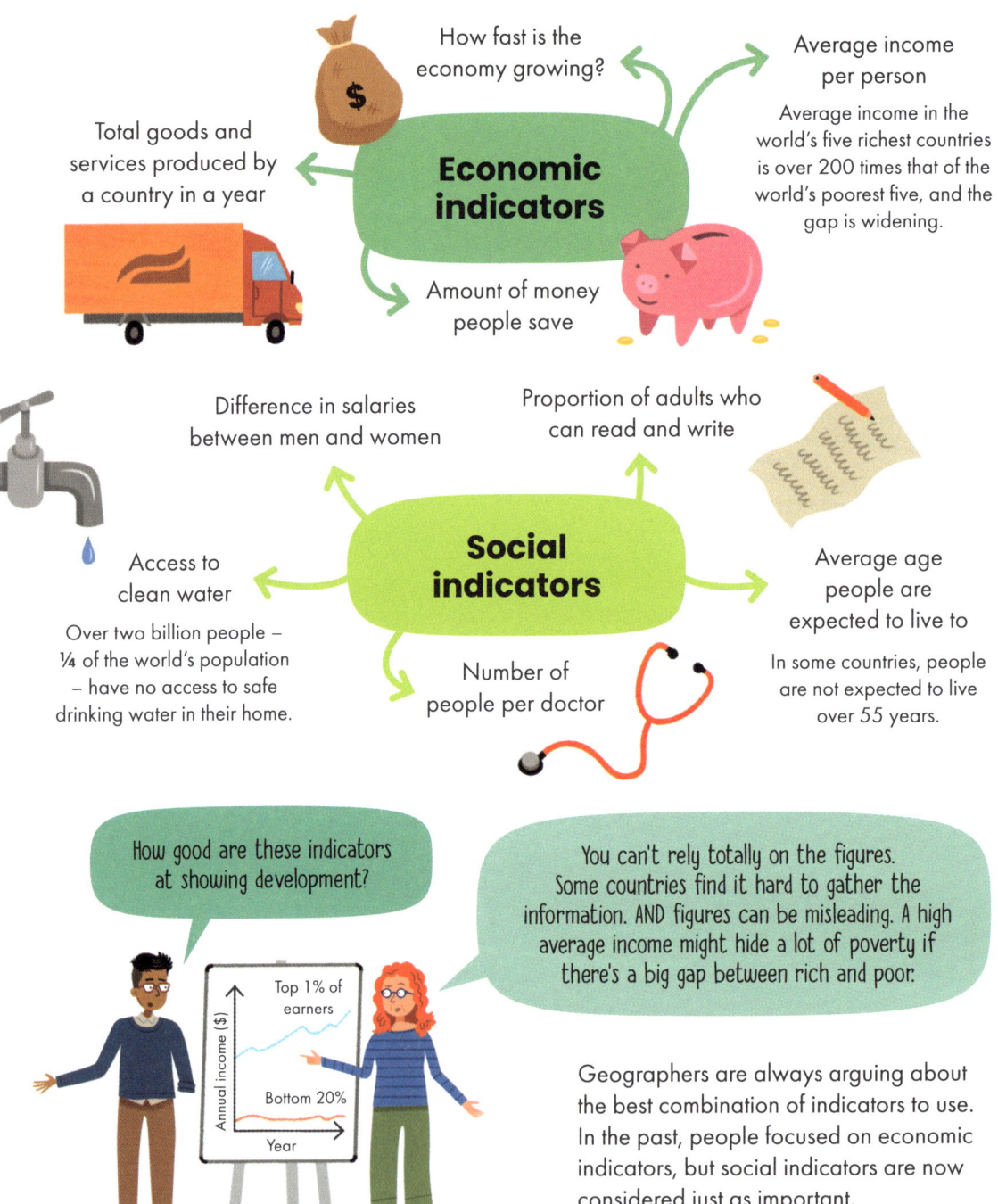

Economic indicators

- How fast is the economy growing?
- Average income per person — Average income in the world's five richest countries is over 200 times that of the world's poorest five, and the gap is widening.
- Total goods and services produced by a country in a year
- Amount of money people save

Social indicators

- Difference in salaries between men and women
- Proportion of adults who can read and write
- Access to clean water — Over two billion people – ¼ of the world's population – have no access to safe drinking water in their home.
- Average age people are expected to live to — In some countries, people are not expected to live over 55 years.
- Number of people per doctor

How good are these indicators at showing development?

You can't rely totally on the figures. Some countries find it hard to gather the information. AND figures can be misleading. A high average income might hide a lot of poverty if there's a big gap between rich and poor.

Geographers are always arguing about the best combination of indicators to use. In the past, people focused on economic indicators, but social indicators are now considered just as important.

Human development index

In 1990, the United Nations created a measure known as the **Human Development Index** (HDI). It aims to show the likelihood of people living a healthy life, with a good education and a decent standard of living.

The HDI is based on four indicators:

- Average age people are expected to live to
- Expected number of years of schooling
- Average years of schooling
- Average income per person

Here's a ranking of places, based on their HDI scores in 2022.

1.	SWITZERLAND	0.962
2.	NORWAY	0.961
3.	ICELAND	0.959
4.	HONG KONG	0.952
5.	AUSTRALIA	0.951
6.	DENMARK	0.948
7.	SWEDEN	0.947
8.	IRELAND	0.945
9.	GERMANY	0.942
10.	NETHERLANDS	0.941

A high HDI rating means people have a high standard of living, healthcare and education, and the opportunity to earn a good income.

In general, countries in Northern Europe have the highest scores, while African countries have the lowest.*

The highest possible HDI score is 1.

*Find out one reason why on page 107.

The HDI is useful for comparing development around the world. However, it ignores many important factors, such as the *rate* of economic growth, freedom or even *happiness*. Some geographers think happiness and wellbeing should be valued more. But how do you measure happiness?

Do you have a few minutes to answer some questions about happiness?

HAPPINESS SURVEY

FROM 1-10, HOW SATISFIED ARE YOU WITH YOUR LIFE? ☐

FROM 1-10, HOW ANXIOUS DID YOU FEEL YESTERDAY? ☐

FROM 1-10, HOW IS YOUR WORK-HOME LIFE BALANCE? ☐

Barriers to development

Some countries remain near the bottom of the HDI list, year after year, no matter how many goods they export or how many social measures they introduce. Geographers investigate the reasons why.

Being landlocked

Sea travel is the cheapest way to transport goods in bulk, so having no access to the coast can raise the cost of trade considerably.

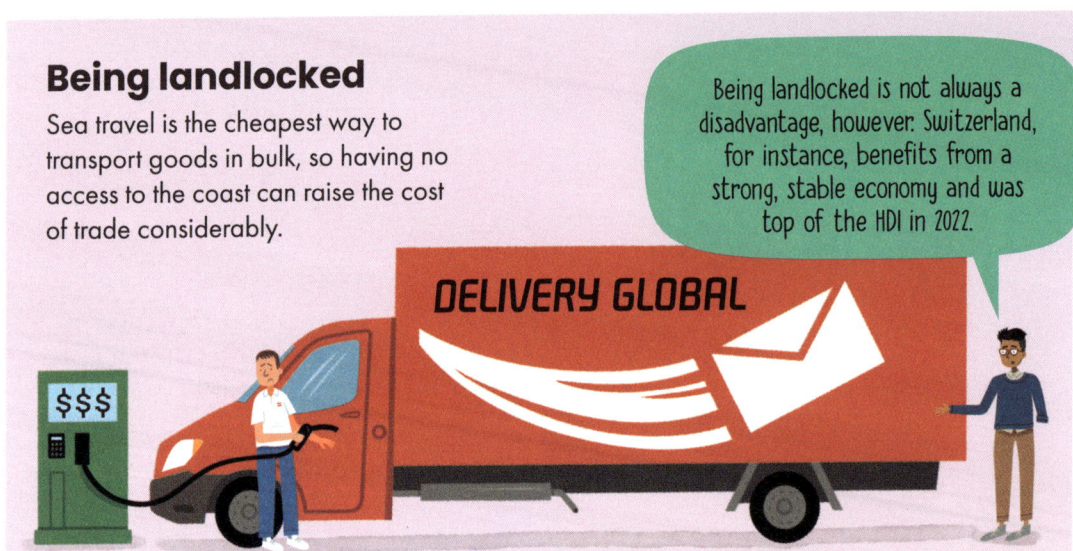

Being landlocked is not always a disadvantage, however. Switzerland, for instance, benefits from a strong, stable economy and was top of the HDI in 2022.

Bad connections

Poor roads and rail links make it harder to do business and make money.

There's been a landslide. Sorry, please turn around.

Overdependence on natural resources

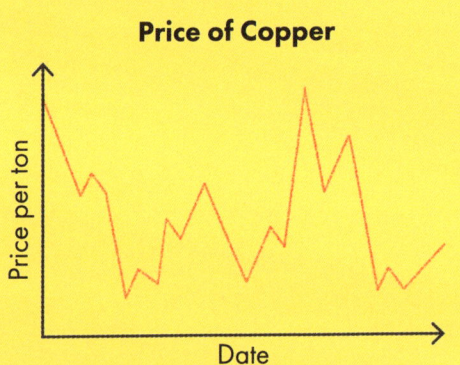

Price of Copper

Some countries make a lot of their income from selling natural resources, such as copper or coffee.

If the price drops, then their income will take a big hit. Countries that sell lots of *different* things will be less affected.

Debt

Many countries borrow money to pay for development projects, such as building schools or roads. The money owed – **debt** – is paid back in regular amounts. Over time, the debt can build up so much it leaves countries with nothing left to spend on basic needs.

Many less-developed countries are struggling to pay back billions of dollars in debt to wealthier countries.

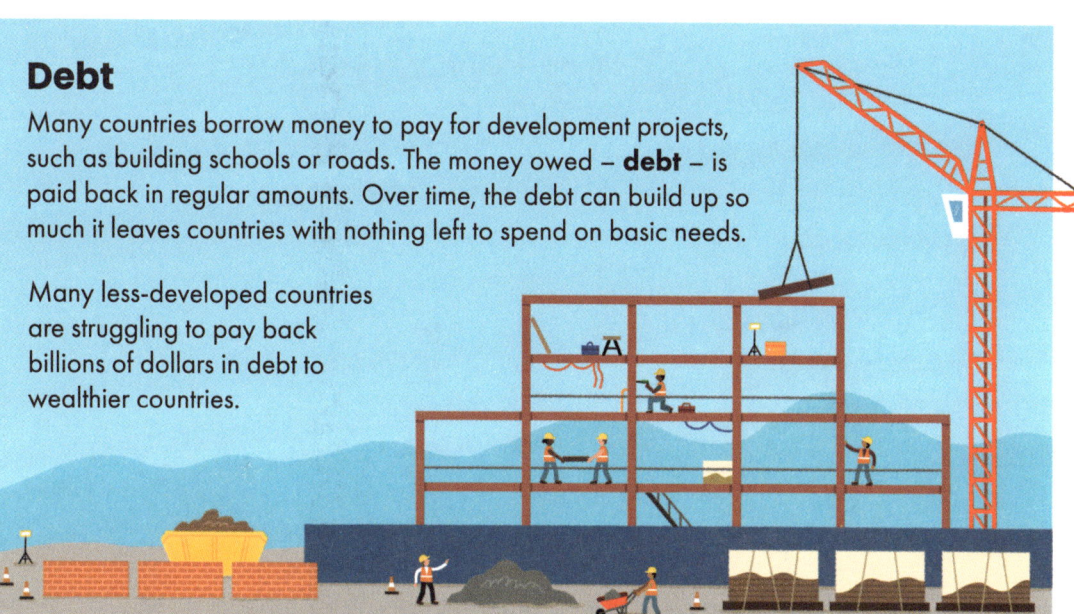

This can lead them into further debt or trade deals that may not be in their best interest over the long term, such as selling oil or gas production to foreign countries.

Weak government

Some governments fail to stop officials from taking bribes or stealing public money that could benefit the country. This is known as **corruption**.

War

War has devastating effects on the economy, education, healthcare and people's lives, forcing many to flee.

Climate and natural disasters

Some countries face crises due to their geographical location. For example, in recent years, Bangladesh and Pakistan have been hit by cyclones and flooding, Ethiopia and Somalia by drought, Ecuador and Haiti by earthquakes and Tonga by a volcanic eruption.

Some of these disasters have been made worse by the climate crisis.

Ending poverty

Many countries, global organizations and charities are working to end poverty and inequality in the world. They focus on **sustainable development** – development that improves people's lives in a lasting way, without harming the needs of future generations.

No one expects geographers to end poverty, but it IS part of their job to gather and map all kinds of data that relates to poverty, including drought, floods, armed conflict, gender inequality and the progress of development projects.

Drought map

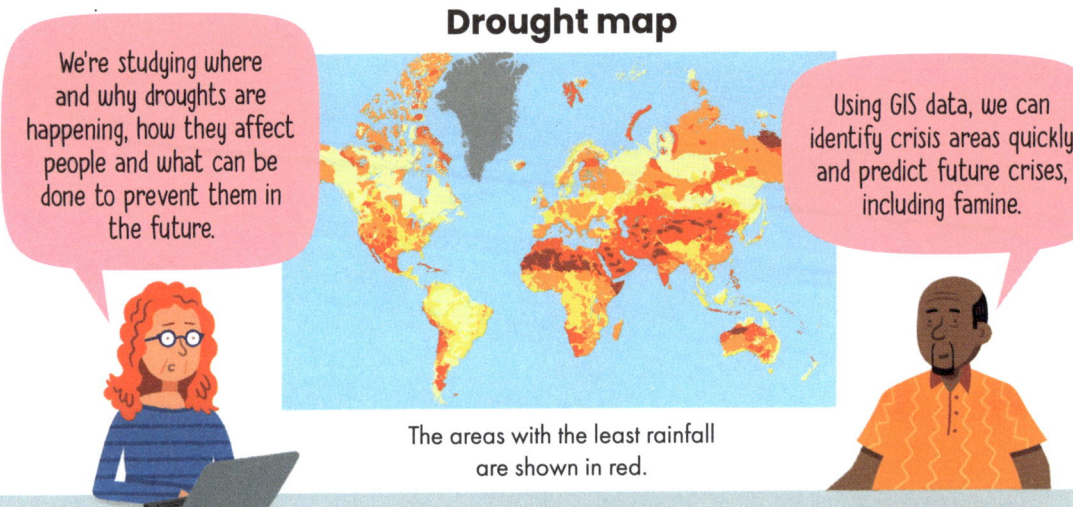

We're studying where and why droughts are happening, how they affect people and what can be done to prevent them in the future.

Using GIS data, we can identify crisis areas quickly and predict future crises, including famine.

The areas with the least rainfall are shown in red.

Geographers look at links between poverty and lack of education. They examine education projects – such as a UN one to build rural classrooms and train teachers in Papua and West Papua, Indonesia – to see the difference they make.

Part of the UN project involved encouraging more girls to go to schools.

Gender equality in education leads to more women in jobs and government, which in turn leads to better family health and a stronger economy. This reduces poverty.

Aid: good or bad?

Often, the quickest way to help with an emergency is to provide money, food or equipment, known as **humanitarian aid**. This happens a lot when conflict or natural disasters strike. But what's the long-term impact?

In 2022, severe drought and conflict in Somalia caused hundreds of thousands of people to leave their homes.

Many of these people faced malnutrition or starvation. Countries and organizations responded by providing aid: food parcels, doctors, medicine and shelter.

Does aid work?

Aid has had major success in reducing poverty and starvation, preventing and curing life-threatening diseases, setting up schools and encouraging more women to get into education and work.

But some countries receive so much aid they become dependent on it. And this prevents them from finding long-term solutions.

True, but we still have to respond to people in need when disasters strike.

Yes, but there's so much more we can do. Take drought, for instance. If we invested more in projects to conserve water and to resolve conflicts around access to water, we'd increase people's ability to cope during water shortages.

Yes, that's a really good idea. But we'll never be able to prevent ALL emergency situations and natural disasters.

CHAPTER 7
Big issues

The world is so big and complex that there's a never-ending supply of questions for geographers to get stuck into. Here are just a few.

> How do you study the geography of a virtual place – like the World Wide Web?

> How much have we humans changed the very planet we live on?

> What if there were no borders?

> Do you think cities would look different if they had been designed by women?

> How can geography tell us about history? And how does history affect today's geography?

> Will we ever find a way to create the perfect map?

Humans changing the planet

Humans are having a dramatic effect on the Earth – so significant, that geologists can *see* it in the ground itself.

Geologists divide the history of the Earth into massive chunks of time. The biggest chunks, known as **eons**, last for hundreds of millions of years. Other chunks, known as **epochs**, last from around 2 to 50 million years.

This diagram shows layers of earth through time split into epochs.

About 12,000 years ago, temperatures rise, and ice sheets covering Earth begin to melt. This marks the start of the most recent epoch, known as the **Holocene**.

Humans start here, about 300,000 years ago

2.58 million years ago, large parts of Earth's Northern Hemisphere become covered with ice. This marks the beginning of the **Pleistocene** epoch.

Geologists look for clues in the ground, such as different kinds of rocks, fossils, ancient ice or particles from the ocean floor that show when one epoch changes into another.

This boundary marks the point when dinosaurs become extinct 66 million years ago, at the end of the **late Cretaceous** epoch.

Reptiles dominate the land. The first plants with flowers appear.

This boundary marks the beginning of the **early Jurassic** epoch, about 200 million years ago.

Mammals appear about 210 million years ago. The first dinosaur fossils are found in rocks about 230 million years old.

Some scientists now say that humans are changing the planet *so much* that a new epoch has begun: the **Anthropocene**. But geologists are still debating whether there is enough hard evidence in the ground for a new epoch.

What evidence *is* there for the Anthropocene and when do people think it began?

That's a good question! Scientists have different opinions about it. Here are some of the dates they suggest...

Present day

1945-1950 Radioactive particles from nuclear bombs are detected in the soil. A surge in global industry and farming leads to widespread habitat destruction and chemicals in the soil. Plastic and concrete waste increases.

1800 A huge rise in coal-fired factories releasing carbon and methane gases into the atmosphere causes pollution and sets off global heating.

1492 Christopher Columbus lands in the Bahamas, sparking a mass movement of people, plants and animals between Europe and the Americas. American remains are found in Europe and vice versa.

4,000-6,000 years ago Farmers clear forests, plant crops and raise animals. This changes the Earth's landscape and releases greenhouse gases into the atmosphere.

It's still not clear that the Anthropocene is a true epoch. The debate about it, however, and its focus on scientific evidence has sparked huge interest from people around the world who are concerned with the future of the planet.

Geography through time

Some geographers are interested in what places were like in the past. They investigate the landscape, the climate and how people lived there. It's an area of study known as **historical geography**.

I'm finding out about the Incas. They lived in the Andes mountains, and ruled an empire that stretched from Ecuador to Chile during the 15th century.

● Inca empire

Ecuador
Peru
Bolivia
Chile
Argentina

3,000m (10,000ft) above sea level

High up in the mountains, where temperatures regularly drop below freezing, experts have uncovered a system of old terraces cut into the hillside.

The terraces show the Incas developed a form of vertical farming that allowed them to grow crops in a sustainable way.

Terrace wall: 2-5m (7-16ft) high

Each terrace was secured with a stone wall, to stop soil from slipping down the slope.

The terraces, known as *andenes*, created flat areas that allowed more sunlight and rain to reach crops and kept plant roots insulated in cold weather.

A zig-zagging system of irrigation canals brought melting ice water from nearby glaciers onto the slopes. Water was also stored in stone tanks, known as **cisterns.**

Historical geographers make use of information from lots of different sources.

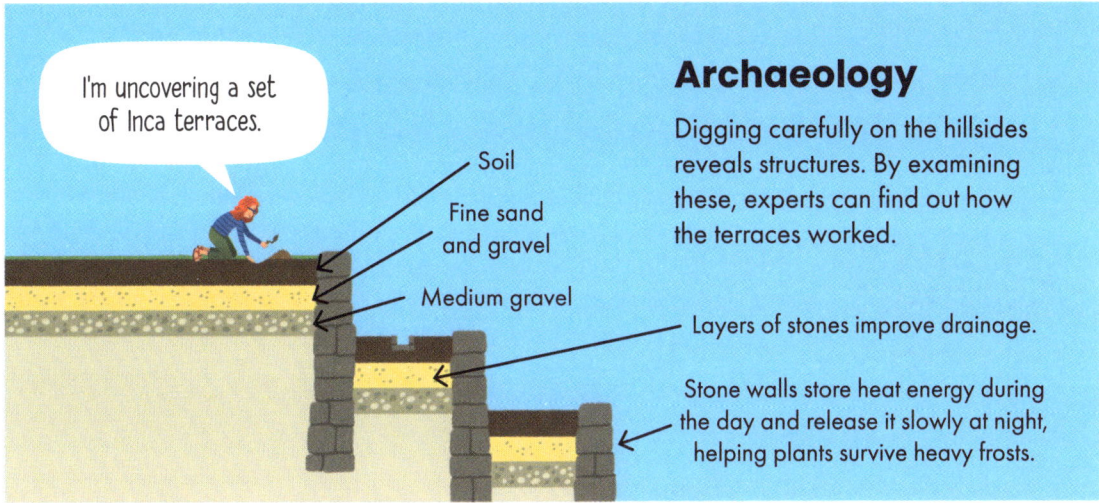

Archaeology

Digging carefully on the hillsides reveals structures. By examining these, experts can find out how the terraces worked.

"I'm uncovering a set of Inca terraces."

- Soil
- Fine sand and gravel
- Medium gravel
- Layers of stones improve drainage.
- Stone walls store heat energy during the day and release it slowly at night, helping plants survive heavy frosts.

Scientific research

Research into pollen, seeds and plant remains shows what kind of crops the Incas grew.

Chemical analysis of the soil shows how they improved thin highland soil with fertile soil from drained flooded land.

"The Incas developed hardy crops that survived frost, drought and flooding. One variety of potato, known as *huaña*, could be soaked, frozen, dried, and then stored for years."

Historical accounts

Written records provide another insight into the Incas' way of life.

The Incas had no system of writing. But Garcilaso de la Vega, the son of an Inca noblewoman and a Spanish conquistador, wrote about their farming skills in a book called *Royal Commentaries of the Incas* in 1609.

"This book describes how the whole hill was gradually transformed to grow crops and the platforms flattened out like stairs in a staircase."

Power and the past

From the 15th century, many European countries began to take control of, or **colonize**, other parts of the world. Over the next few hundred years, global politics was dominated by just a few European powers. This has had a huge impact on world geography.

By the 1700s, much of North, Central, South America and the islands of the Caribbean were controlled by a handful of European countries.

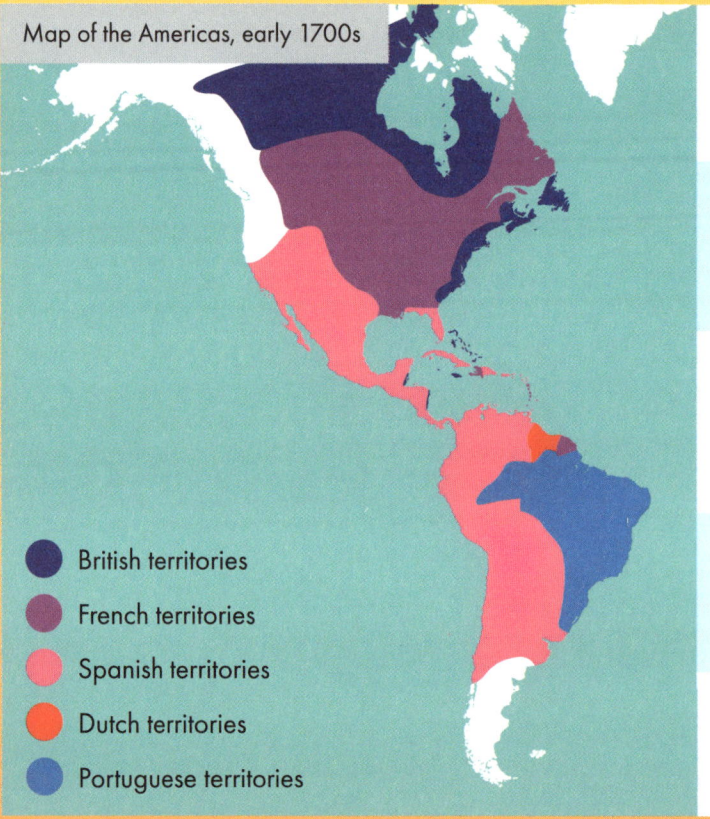

Map of the Americas, early 1700s

- British territories
- French territories
- Spanish territories
- Dutch territories
- Portuguese territories

As Europeans moved to the places they had colonized, they...

...forced their laws, religion and language on the people who lived there.

...built houses, roads, industry and introduced new kinds of medicine, new ways of writing and governing.

...brought deadly diseases such as smallpox, causing millions of deaths.

...took natural resources, such as gold and silver from the territories they ruled.

From the 16th to the 19th centuries, Europeans took millions of people by force from West Africa to the Americas, where they were enslaved and made to work for no pay.

Lasting effects of colonialism

From the 18th century, some colonies began to win back their independence, but many of them still suffer from the complex, lasting effects of colonialism. Indeed, many of the poorest countries today were once colonies.

In the 18th century, Haiti was the richest colony in the world. Since its independence from France in 1804, it has struggled. At first it was forced to pay money to France, and has since suffered from political instability and many natural disasters. Today Haiti is one of the poorest countries in the world.

Many colonizers introduced racist laws and systems which treated people differently depending on how they looked or where they were from.

One effect of colonialism is the blend of cultures and ethnicities across the Americas and throughout the world. Another effect is discrimination against indigenous and Black people.

Many countries have introduced laws against racism. But Black and indigenous people still face more obstacles to jobs, justice and to living healthy, prosperous lives than white people.

In some countries, border lines were drawn by European leaders, without considering the landscape or communities they were dividing. This created tensions between ethnic groups and border disputes which continue to this day.

I'm from Angola, but also part of an ancient culture that speaks Kikongo. We were colonized by Portuguese, French and Belgian settlers.

Today, six million Kikongo speakers are spread between four countries: Angola, the Democratic Republic of the Congo, the Republic of the Congo and Gabon.

107

Spaces and people

You might never have noticed that buildings and spaces can relate to things about YOU as an individual. Some geographers examine how spaces are experienced differently depending on your gender, age, ethnicity or physical ability.

Being aware of the way that different groups of people experience cities can help planners create spaces that are more **inclusive**, or welcoming, for everyone.

When officials in Vienna, Austria, examined who was using their parks in the mid-1990s, they discovered that girls were much less likely to use the parks after the age of nine, while boys continued using them into their teens.

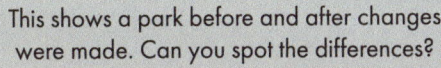
This shows a park before and after changes were made. Can you spot the differences?

After carrying out surveys, park designers added volleyball, netball and badminton courts that were popular with girls. They also added more seating areas for people to stop and socialize more easily.

Why is it important to create inclusive spaces?

If people don't feel safe, welcome or comfortable in a space, they are less likely to use that space. But public spaces are meant to be for everyone.

How easy is it to create inclusive spaces?

It's hard. We often don't realize how other people experience spaces differently.

How can geography help with this?

By doing surveys, research and just watching to see how and why people gather in some spaces and not in others.

Digital world

The **internet** is a collection of computer networks around the world. Ideas, information, money and images can be shared in the blink of an eye across the Earth... and beyond. Digital geographers see it as a unique space where distance, time and location no longer really matter.

One way to map the internet is by drawing lines between networks which are connected. For example, most schools in a city have their own network, and are also connected to a larger local network.

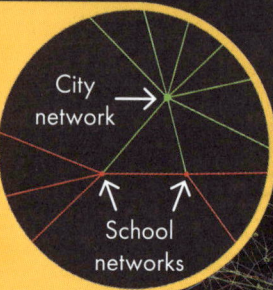

City network

School networks

When you map ALL the connections between ALL the networks across the entire internet, you end up with a gigantic web of criss-crossing lines, which looks a bit like this. ⟶

Brighter areas show which local networks have LOTS of connections to other networks.

Geographers also map the internet's physical parts. These include undersea cables, computers, wifi towers and satellites.

Undersea cable

Countries which have the most undersea cable connections tend to have the fastest and cheapest connections.

Digital geographers also investigate how people and places are shaped by their position in the digital world. Here are some questions they might try to answer.

- How affordable and fast is people's internet connection around the world?
- Which companies dominate the internet, and what consequences does this have?
- How do search engines influence our perception of places?

ASK ME A QUESTION...
Is the UK
Is the UK rainy
Is the UK a country

What is and isn't represented on the internet is sometimes even a question of life and death.

In 2014, when a deadly disease known as Ebola spread through West Africa, it was hard to distribute food and medicine, because large areas were unmapped.

Volunteers stepped in to make digital maps, by tracing over satellite imagery. These helped charities reach the people who needed aid.

111

Who gets to move around?

According to the United Nations' *Universal Declaration of Human Rights*, people should have the right to enter, exit, move around in, and live in any country they choose. But in reality, every country has rules about who gets to do these things.

WELCOME TO ITALY

"I'm Japanese. My passport allows me to visit 200 countries without needing to apply for permission. That's more than any other passport in the world."

"With my European passport, I can move freely between 27 countries of the European Union. So no border checks for me!"

"After getting a job in Italy, I was able to apply for a work permit that allows me to live there."

"I've invested half a million Euros in an Italian business in exchange for a resident's permit."

Without the right paperwork, moving to new countries is *really* difficult.

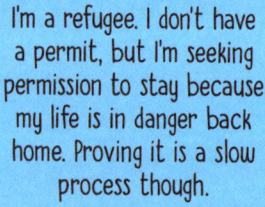

"I'm a refugee. I don't have a permit, but I'm seeking permission to stay because my life is in danger back home. Proving it is a slow process though."

"We're looking for a better life. We couldn't get a permit so we're paying people to help us cross the border in secret."

When it comes to moving around, there are rules for everyone. But these rules are very different depending on where you were born, your skills and your wealth.

Should we open our borders?

A country with **open borders** is one which anyone can freely move to in order to find work. People usually make two kinds of arguments for opening borders.

It will make the world richer.

More people will be able to move abroad for better-paying jobs. This gets them out of poverty and boosts their new country's economy.

But what about the country they leave? Losing workers must hold poorer countries back.

Well, many immigrants send back a chunk of their earnings, and regularly go back. So their home country does benefit.

But what about workers in the new country? They face more competition for jobs and there's less money to go around.

I disagree. Richer countries tend to have more elderly people – they NEED more young workers to get all the jobs done.

Well I'm glad *you're* here, but what if *millions* more come?

It's the right thing to do.

Where you're born is just a matter of luck. If you want to leave, you should be free to. And if you're lucky enough to have been born in a rich country, you have no right to exclude other people from it.

That sounds nice, but what about respecting people's wishes? If most people are against immigration, then their government should listen and not open borders fully.

People are mostly only against open borders because newspapers and politicians sometimes unfairly blame immigrants for the lack of jobs or resources.

But it's not just about money or jobs. I think we need to protect our culture. When people emigrate, they bring their ideas, languages and ways of doing things with them.

To me that sounds like a good thing.

Geographers rarely get to decide how open a border should be, but they can influence the debate. For example, some make predictions about what the world might be like, and what effects it would have, IF people could move freely.

113

Questioning maps

Maps help make sense of the world and reveal patterns and relationships. But for maps to work, many things are often left out, simplified or even made up. It's a map-reader's job to question what's going on.

How accurate is it?

This image of Brasilia is based on a satellite image. It was accurate at the time the photo was taken, but it becomes less so over time.

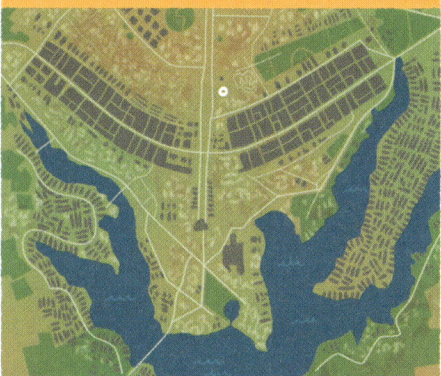

Is what it shows *true*?

What's the source of the map's facts? How trustworthy do you think the map is?

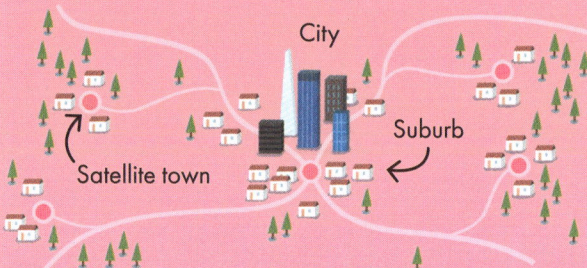

This map from page 62 is of a made-up city. But it's still informative because it shows the different ways cities tend to grow.

Which choices have been made?

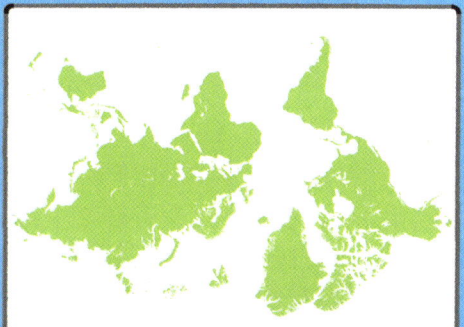

The world isn't flat, North isn't *up*, and Europe isn't in the *middle*. But many maps choose to show the Earth that way. Questioning these accepted mapmaking practices can reshape the way we see the world.

What's been simplified?

Maps simplify reality – this is what makes them useful. But they can make you forget how messy and uncertain the real world is.

This map shows greater Tokyo. The darkest blue patch is the most densely populated region. The map makes the boundaries between the inner and outer areas look clear, but people living on the edges might not agree.

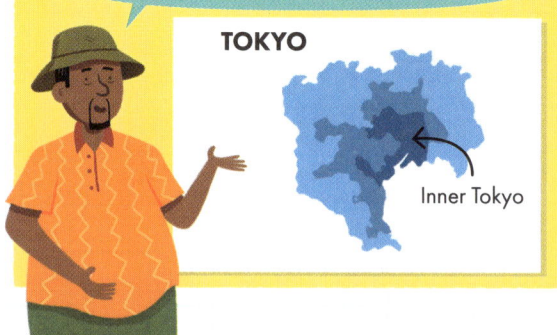

Who made the map?

This map of the Ganges river in South Asia on pages 52-53 was made by a European mapmaker. If local people had made it, how might it be different?

This map doesn't use ANY of the local names for the river: Jahnavi, Shubhra, Sapteshwari, Nikita, Bhagirathi, Alaknanda...

Ganges

Is there anything strange?

Why is the border on the political map of the island of New Guinea so straight?

Western New Guinea (Indonesia)

Papua New Guinea

In the 19th century, the island's English and Dutch colonizers split the island in two along a new artificial line. Maps often reflect the position of people who used to have, or still have, power.

What's the map trying to say?

Every map is trying to convince you of something. For example, using vibrant red to mark out areas of drought on this map emphasizes that it's an important, dangerous problem.

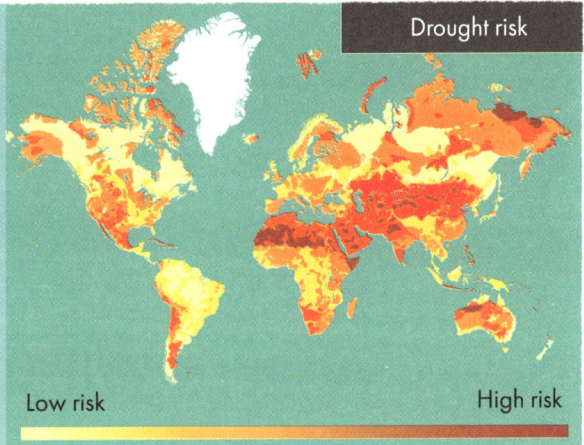

Drought risk

Low risk   High risk

Next time you look at a map, stop and think for a moment about these kinds of questions. They will help you work out if you agree with what the map is trying to say, and how effective and useful it is.

Here and now

How well do you know the place where you live? Here are some ideas for exploring geography right here, right now without having to go anywhere exotic or far away.

First, identify something in your local area that you're curious to find out more about...

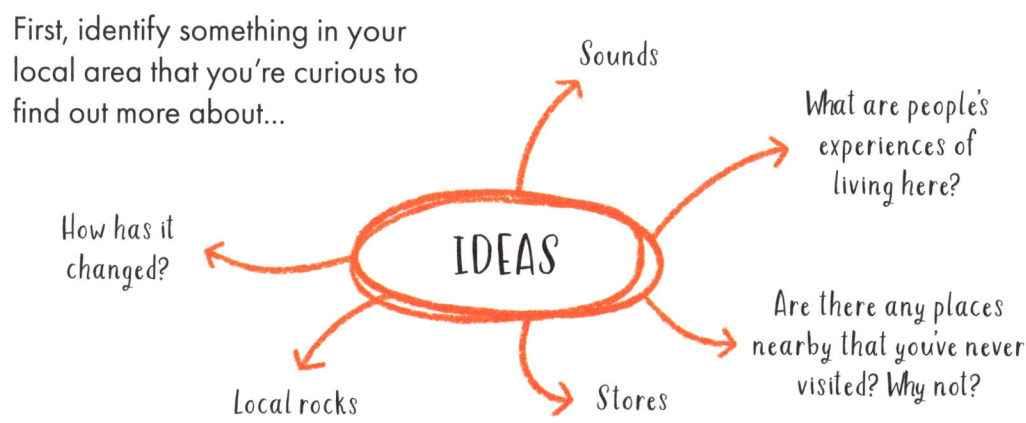

- Sounds
- What are people's experiences of living here?
- How has it changed?
- IDEAS
- Local rocks
- Stores
- Are there any places nearby that you've never visited? Why not?

... then see what you can find out using one or more of the techniques on these pages.

Look it up

Find out more about your chosen topic by visiting a library, looking online or reading books or newspapers.

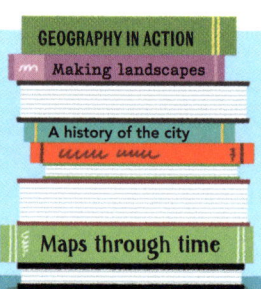

Sketch or photograph

Investigate your topic by taking photos or sketching it. For example, what do you notice about the buildings around you?

Why are these barns no longer used for farming?

Why are there similar places next door to each other?

Is there anything you're surprised NOT to find?

Collect people's stories

Ask people to share their memories, thoughts and feelings about a place. Are there any similar words they use, or themes they pick up on? What are the differences?

let me tell you, our area has changed a lot. It feels less busy, but there's much more traffic!

Search for satellite imagery

Websites such as Google Earth allow you to look at satellite images of any point on Earth. Search for your local area and see if you can spot familiar buildings, roads and green spaces. You might even be able to find something you didn't know was there.

Older satellite images are also available on Google Earth, so you can see how things have changed.

Fun with maps

Another project you can do is to mark up a map. For instance, you could shade in the places that friends or family have visited around the world.

Countries visited by people in my class

Scan this symbol with the camera on a smartphone. It will take you to Usborne Quicklinks, where you can download a world map that you can print out and shade in with pens or pencils.

117

Geography in action

From creating green spaces, to defending ancient customs, people use geography as a tool to bring about change. Here are some examples of geography in action to get you inspired.

Mapping a refugee camp

Palestinian refugees living in a camp in Lebanon found they had very limited space. With help from a local charity, they sent up balloons with cameras attached.

The pictures from those cameras helped them make detailed maps. In turn, those maps helped identify suitable areas where people in the camp could grow food and mark out green spaces.

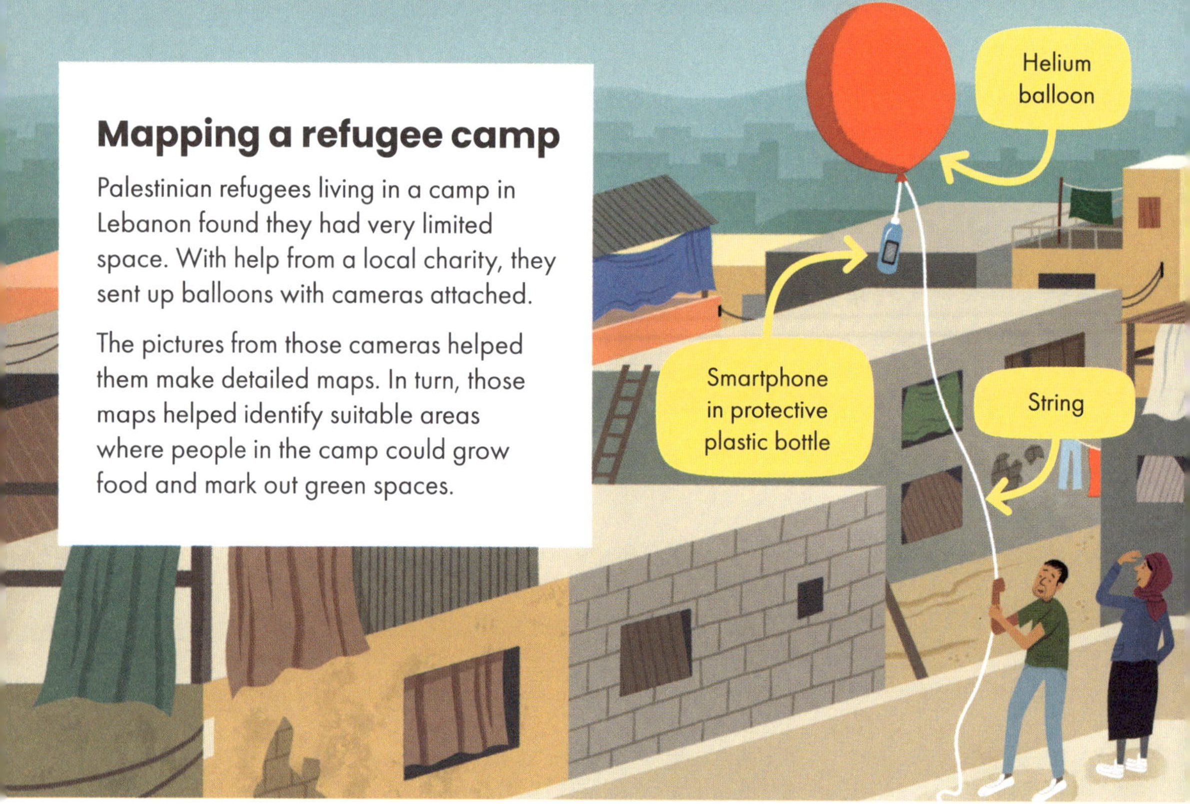

Helium balloon

Smartphone in protective plastic bottle

String

Fighting for rights

The **right to roam** is an ancient custom that allows anyone to wander in open countryside. In some countries, such as Norway and Estonia, this right is protected by law. But in many countries it isn't.

We're campaigning to get this right recognized in the UK.

RIGHT TO ROAM!

Protecting a whole country

Situated at the mouth of three major rivers, and partly under sea level, the Netherlands is constantly threatened by floods. It's home to one of the most complex flood control projects in the world – managed by elected geographers working in special Water Councils. Over the last few decades, they've built structures along the coast and rivers to prevent water from pouring inland.

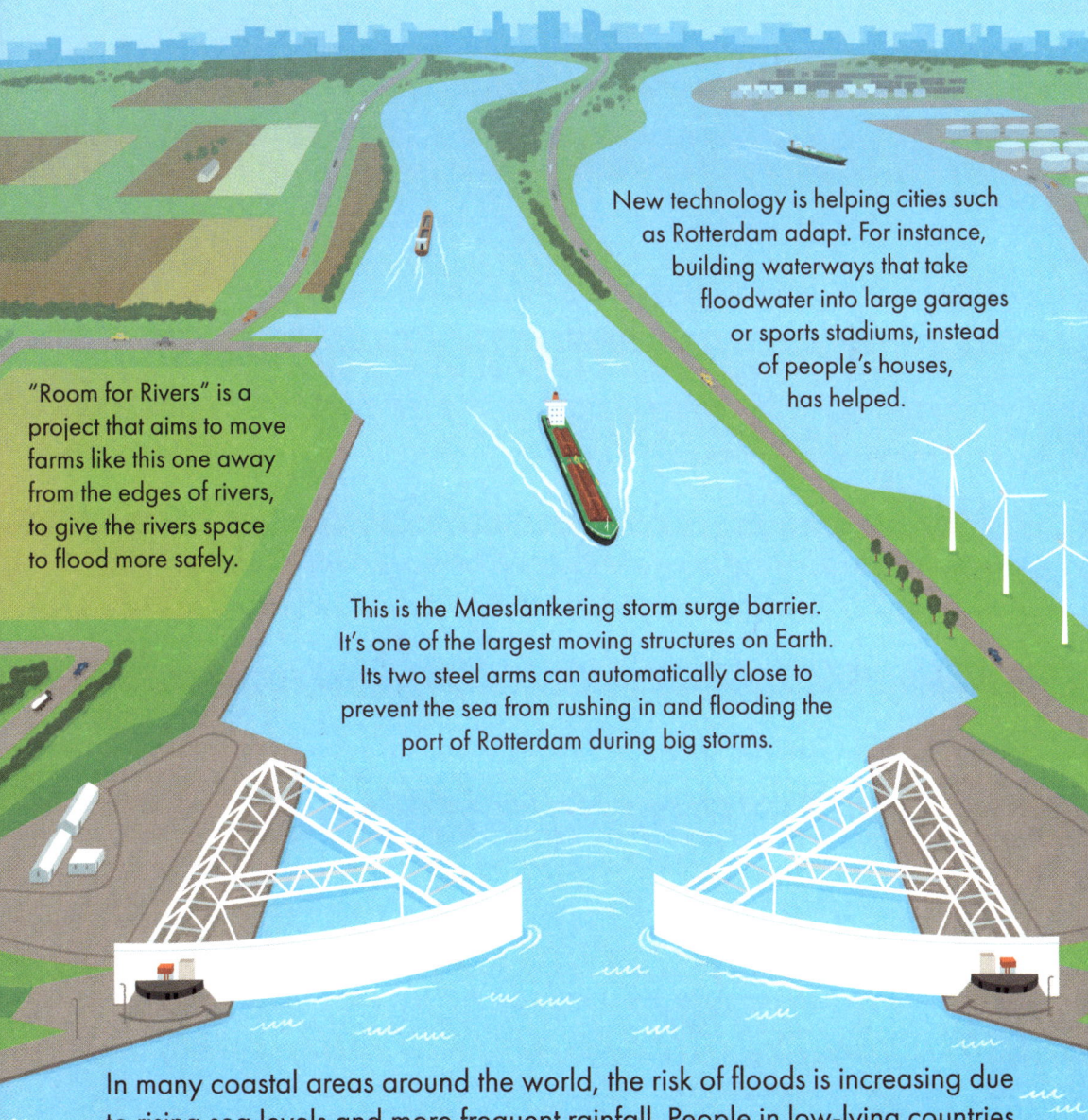

"Room for Rivers" is a project that aims to move farms like this one away from the edges of rivers, to give the rivers space to flood more safely.

New technology is helping cities such as Rotterdam adapt. For instance, building waterways that take floodwater into large garages or sports stadiums, instead of people's houses, has helped.

This is the Maeslantkering storm surge barrier. It's one of the largest moving structures on Earth. Its two steel arms can automatically close to prevent the sea from rushing in and flooding the port of Rotterdam during big storms.

In many coastal areas around the world, the risk of floods is increasing due to rising sea levels and more frequent rainfall. People in low-lying countries such as the Netherlands face tough choices in the future. Should they keep building barriers, or just move away from the most risky areas?

Geography is *EVERYWHERE!*

Geography is *everywhere* and *all around*.
It's a WAY of looking at the world which can help you
make sense of it, take action and make a difference.
So get out there and BE a geographer!

That means tuning in to how spaces shape us, and how we shape spaces.

You might notice things that need fixing...

...opportunities

Glossary

This glossary explains some of the words used in this book.
Words in *italics* are explained in other entries.

atmosphere a layer of gases around the Earth, including oxygen.

biome a type of region with a particular *climate* where certain varieties of plants or animals live, such as a desert or rainforest.

cartographer someone who makes maps.

census an official count of people and households. It helps governments plan housing, health and other services.

climate the usual pattern of weather in a region.

colonization when one country takes control of another country or territory and its people settle there.

conservation protecting things for the future, for instance an area of land, oceans, animals or old buildings.

crust the outer layer of planet Earth.

data information, including facts, surveys and measurements, used for research.

deforestation cutting down a large area of trees.

demography the study of human populations, for instance the birth rate or health of a population.

development a branch of geography that examines people's standard of living and quality of life.

drought a lack of rainfall for an extended period of time.

epidemiology a way of looking at how diseases spread in different regions.

equator a circle of *latitude* that divides the Earth into two halves: the northern and southern *hemispheres*.

erosion the wearing away of earth or rocks by natural forces, such as wind, rain or rivers.

European Union an alliance of 27 countries in Europe that share rules of trade and security.

fossil the remains of an ancient plant or animal that has turned to stone and is preserved in rock.

fossil fuel a substance, such as oil, coal or gas, that comes from the remains of buried plants and animals that died millions of years ago. It is burned to make energy.

geology the study of rocks and Earth's history, including physical processes such as earthquakes and volcanoes.

GIS short for geographical information system. GIS is a system that gathers and maps all kinds of information on a single image.

glacier a large body of ice that moves slowly down a mountain slope or river valley.

globalization the connection between people and places all over the world, through trade, music, art, social media, the internet.

greenhouse gas a gas in the *atmosphere*, such as carbon dioxide, that absorbs heat from the Earth. Greenhouse gases can build up and increase the Earth's temperature.

Greenwich meridian a circle of *longitude* around Earth from the North pole to the South pole. It passes through the Royal Observatory in Greenwich, London.

hemisphere half of the Earth, such as the northern hemisphere.

Human development index a measure of human development based on life expectancy, education and income.

igneous a type of rock made from cooled magma or lava, such as granite or basalt.

immigration when people move to a new country to live there permanently.

indigenous the inhabitants of a place before colonizers or settlers arrive.

latitude a measure that shows the distance of a place north or south of the *equator*.

longitude a measure that shows the distance of a place east or west of the *Greenwich Meridian*.

magma molten hot rock from beneath the Earth's surface.

mantle a thick layer inside Earth below the *crust*.

megacity a city of more than 10 million people.

metamorphic rocks that have changed significantly after intense heat or pressure, for instance slate or marble.

meteorology the study of the *atmosphere*, in particular to forecast the *weather*.

migration a long journey of people or animals from one place to another.

natural resources things found in nature that people use, for instance, soil, fossil fuels, water, trees, diamonds, lithium, iron ore.

population the number of people living in a particular place.

refugee a person who is forced to leave their country due to war or other dangers, and seeks refuge – safety – in a new country.

renewable energy energy created from natural sources that won't run out, such as the wind, sun, oceans.

reservoir an artificial lake to store water.

Ring of fire a name for the ring of volcanoes around the rim of the Pacific Ocean.

rock cycle the forming of different kinds of rocks changing over time.

rural a countryside area outside cities or towns.

sedimentary rocks made from layers of sand, mud or grit, that have been squashed together over time.

seismometer a machine that picks up movements or sounds caused by earthquakes, volcanoes or explosions.

statistics studying and making sense of *data*.

suburb an outer residential area of a city.

superpower a powerful country with lots of influence over world affairs.

surveyor someone who makes precise measurements of the land. They are useful for fixing boundaries, making maps and building work.

temperate a temperate *climate* has moderate *weather* with no extremes of heat, cold, rainfall or *drought*.

United Nations an international organization made up of nearly every country in the world. It aims to promote world peace and reduce poverty and inequality.

urban relating to a city or town.

weather the state of the *atmosphere* in a particular place, including the temperature and whether it is sunny or rainy, for example.

Jobs in geography

Geography involves working with numbers, words, maps and people. It overlaps with all kinds of subjects. Few people have the job title of geographer, but it's the way into *all types* of jobs. Here are just a few.

Town planner

Town planners design and manage towns and cities. They look at the big picture – from building houses and expanding green areas to improving road or rail networks.

Landscape designer

Landscape designers get involved in individual projects to improve streets, buildings, parks and gardens.

I'm designing an urban walkway and the space around a canal.

Nature conservationist

If you love the outdoors, you might want to educate people about it and work on projects to protect it – from maintaining paths to planting trees and rescuing wildlife.

Cartographer

If you're fascinated by maps, you might want to get involved in making them. Cartographers make maps of just about anything. They sometimes work with GIS analysts who analyze trends and patterns using digital maps.

I'm an epidemiologist. I look at patterns of diseases on maps to help investigate health issues.

Surveyor

Land surveyors measure the land, collect data on buildings, hills, rivers and borders, and make accurate site plans – useful in lots of industries.

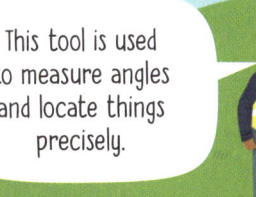

I look at the value of land and advise businesses on whether it's cheaper to expand in one location or move to a new location.

This tool is used to measure angles and locate things precisely.

Environmental consultant

Environmental consultants advise on the risk to places from storms and climate change and look at ways to make businesses more eco-friendly.

I collect data on flood risk, waste disposal from water companies and sea pollution.

Politics

A big part of geography is collecting data about how people live. That's vital work for all kinds of political groups, from local councils to international organizations dedicated to improving lives.

Mining

Lots of jobs in mining involve geographical skills. Geological engineers design mines and explore sites for drilling, hydrologists advise on protecting groundwater and seismologists study ground movements.

Energy

Geographical skills are useful in all parts of the energy industry, from wind, solar and tidal energy to nuclear, oil and gas.

I'm a photojournalist. I've been taking photographs of the Zambezi River to show how much fresh water is disappearing due to construction projects.

Index

Addis Ababa, 11
Africa, 10, 22-23, 67, 68, 82, 84, 106, 111
aid, 99
Amazon, 43
Andes, 42, 104-105
Angola, 107
animals, 16, 17, 40, 43, 48-49, 102-103
Anthropocene, 103
Asia, 52, 57, 67, 84
atmosphere, 30-33, 103
Australia, 36
Austria, 109

Bangladesh, 53, 97
biomes, 42, 43
birth rates, 66, 67, 68
Belgium, 79
Bolivia, 78
borders, 77, 78-79, 107, 112, 113
Brazil, 63, 81
butterfly effect, 35

Canada, 60, 61
Caribbean, 106, 107
cartographers, 124
China, 53, 68
cities, 43, 57, 60-73, 75, 108-109, 114, 124
climate, 6, 31, 38-42, 48, 52, 83, 97
climate change see climate crisis
climate crisis, 12, 27, 29, 39, 40, 87, 97, 103
colonialism, 106-107
continents, 16, 17
coordinates, 11
countries, 78-79
countryside, 57, 74-75, 118
culture, 7, 69, 84, 85, 86
currents, magnetic, 18

currents, ocean, 48
cyclones, see hurricanes

data, 9, 12, 34-35, 93-95, 98
debt, 97
demographers, 6
Denmark, 72, 73
deserts, 42, 54
development, 7, 93-99
diseases, 5, 13, 83, 99, 106, 111
droughts, 54, 97, 98, 99, 115

earth scientists, 6
Earth, structure of, 11, 15, 18, 20
earthquakes, 19, 21, 24, 97
economies, 69, 82, 83, 89, 94, 96, 97, 98, 113
education, 66, 93, 94, 95, 97, 98, 99
Ethiopia, 11, 97
equator, 11, 38
emissions, 41
energy, 27, 28, 29, 41, 45, 53, 82, 83, 125
erosion, 8, 41
Estonia, 118
Europe, 40, 66, 81, 84, 95, 106
European Union (EU), 89

farming, 5, 6, 43, 58-59, 103
flooding, 5, 12, 36, 41, 51, 119
food, 5, 22, 40, 43, 54, 66, 74, 99, 118
forests, 42, 43, 103
fossil fuels, 27, 28, 39
fossils, 17, 102
Ganges, 52-53, 115
geography, types of:
 economic, 7, 65-67

 digital, 110-111
 environmental, 6, 22-23, 42-43, 50-51, 125
 political, 7, 97, 112-113, 125
 rural, 6, 74-75
 urban, 6, 60-72
geology, 6, 16-29
Giant's Causeway, 24
GIS, 12, 37, 98, 124
global heating, 33, 39, 41, 103
globalization, 84-87
governments, 7, 66, 70, 74, 77, 78, 83, 97, 98, 113
greenhouse gases, 33, 103
Greenwich meridian, 11

Haiti, 97, 107
happiness, 95
health, 13, 66, 93
Himalayas, 20, 52
history, 83, 101, 102-107
hotspots, 20
Human Development Index (HDI), 95
hurricanes, 36-37, 97
hydrologists, 6, 125

ice, 16, 17, 24, 25, 39, 40, 50, 51
immigrants, 90, 91, 113
India, 52, 79, 90
indicators, 94-95
indigenous people, 43, 107
Indonesia, 98, 115
industry, 62, 63, 68, 82, 103
informal settlements, 63
internet, 9, 59, 75, 85, 110-111
islands, 51, 79
Italy, 5, 63

Japan, 40
jobs, 6, 7, 124-125

Kiribati, 51
Kosovo, 78, 79

126

latitude, 11, 42
lava, 23, 24
life expectancy, 7, 66, 67
   94-95
longitude, 11
London, 11, 67

Madagascar, 79
magma, 21
magnetic poles, 18
Mali, 63
maps, 8, 10-13, 20, 21, 37,
   48-49, 63, 101, 110, 114,
   115, 117, 118, 124
   physical, 42
   political, 78-79
Mariana Trench, 21
megacities, 67, 68
metals, 22, 26, 28
meteorology, 7, 27, 31
Mexico, 78
migration, 90
mines, 22, 29, 125
mountains, 20, 25, 38, 42,
   47, 48, 104
Myanmar, 36

natural disasters, 21, 36,
   40, 51, 67, 91, 97, 99,
   107
natural gas, 26, 27, 81,
   82, 125
Norway, 118
Netherlands, the, 79, 119
New Guinea, 98, 115
New York, 51, 67, 70
Nigeria, 68, 82-83
Niyarogongo, 22-23
North America, 66, 106
nuclear power, 27, 125

oceans, 16, 47, 48-49
   Arctic, 40, 50
   Atlantic, 10
   Pacific, 10, 20-21,
      40, 49
oil, 26, 27, 68, 77, 82, 125
Øresund Bridge, 72-73

ozone layer, 32

plastic, 26, 28, 53,
   54, 103
politics, 7, 70, 77, 125
pollution, 53, 67, 70, 71,
   103
population, 6, 9, 55, 57,
   60-68, 74, 78, 79, 83,
   88, 113
poverty, 7, 92, 94, 95,
   98-99
projections, 10

quality of life, 70, 71, 93,
   94-95
Qatar, 55

rainforests, 42, 43
refugees, 91, 112, 118
regeneration, 65
ridges, 21
Rio Grande, 78
rivers, 5, 8, 46, 47, 55, 65,
   78, 82
rock cycle, 25
rocks, 6, 8, 15, 17, 22,
   23, 24-29, 46, 47, 102
rural areas, 57, 74
Russia, 79, 81

satellite imagery, 12, 117
satellite towns, 62
Saudi Arabia, 38, 90
sea levels, 40, 41, 50-51,
   53, 119
seas, 17, 21, 25, 36, 38, 48
Seoul, 65
Sheldon, Joan, 39
slave trade, 106
Snow, John 13
soil, 5, 22, 46, 47, 52,
   54, 74, 103, 105
solar panels, 26, 28
Somalia, 97, 99
South America, 42, 104
space, 32, 33, 46
Spain, 69
Spilhaus, Athelstan, 48

storms, 5, 36, 119
suburbs, 62
Sun, the, 28, 32, 38, 47
superpowers, 77, 88-89
surveys, 9, 74, 75, 94-95,
   108, 109
Sweden, 72, 73
Switzerland, 82-83, 96

technology, 12, 28, 85, 119
tectonic plates, 16, 17,
   20-21, 25
Tokyo, 64, 67, 114
tornadoes, 36
town planners, 65, 71, 125
towns, 59, 60, 66, 68
trade, 5, 63, 80-81, 84, 85,
   86, 89, 96, 97
trenches, 21
tsunamis, 21
typhoons, *see* hurricanes

Ukraine, 81
United Arab Emirates (UAE),
   90
United Kingdom (UK), 66
United Nations (UN), 89, 95,
   98, 112
United States (US), 37, 78,
   88, 90

Vatican City, 61
Vietnam, 38
villages, 9, 59, 75
volcanic eruptions, 17, 20-21,
   22-23, 97
volcanoes, 5, 22-23, 25

wars, 80, 88, 89, 91, 97
water, 6, 8, 16, 25, 36, 40,
   45-55, 94, 104, 119, 125
water cycle, 47
weather, 7, 31-43, 47, 48,
   104
wind turbines, 28
women and geography, 94,
   98, 101, 108-109
world maps, 10, 11, 18, 20, 40,
   52, 78-79, 98, 117

127

Acknowledgements

Written by
Minna Lacey, Lara Bryan
& Sarah Hull

Edited by
Alex Frith

Illustrated by
Wesley Robins

Designed by
Samuel Gorham & Freya Harrison

Cartography by Craig Asquith

Series designer:
Stephen Moncrieff

Series editor:
Jane Chisholm

Geography expert:
Dr. Roger Trend

Diversity consultants:
Show Racism the Red Card

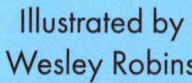

The websites recommended at Usborne Quicklinks are regularly reviewed but Usborne Publishing is not responsible and does not accept liability for the availability or content of any website other than its own, or for any exposure to harmful, offensive or inaccurate material which may appear on the Web. Usborne Publishing will have no liability for any damage or loss caused by viruses that may be downloaded as a result of browsing the sites it recommends.

First published in 2023 by Usborne Publishing Limited,
83–85 Saffron Hill, London EC1N 8RT, United Kingdom.
usborne.com

Copyright © 2023 Usborne Publishing Limited. The name Usborne and the Balloon logo are registered trade marks of Usborne Publishing Limited. All rights reserved.
No part of this publication may be reproduced, stored in a retrieval system or transmitted in any form or by any means without the prior permission of the publisher. UE